# MUD, SONGS AND BLIGHTY

## —A Scrapbook of the First World War—

### Compiled by Colin Walsh

HUTCHINSON OF LONDON

Hutchinson & Co (Publishers) Ltd
3 Fitzroy Square, London W1

London Melbourne Sydney Auckland
Wellington Johannesburg and agencies
throughout the world

First published 1975
This arrangement ©Colin Walsh 1975

Songs© copyright for all territories
See details on individual songs
Reproduced by arrangement with EMI Music Publishing Ltd
'Keep The Home Fires Burning' (Novello/Guilbert Ford)
reproduced by permission of Ascerberg, Hopwood
and Crew Limited and by arrangement with Chappell and Co. Ltd

The First World War song postcards reproduced
in this book were produced by Bamforth and Co. Ltd.,
of Holmfirth, Yorkshire. The life models were local
inhabitants and the backcloths were painted by the
founder of the firm, Mr. James Bamforth. The firm is
still one of the leading publishers of postcards in the country.

Printed in Great Britain by The Anchor Press Ltd,
and bound by Wm Brendon & Son Ltd,
both of Tiptree, Essex

ISBN 0 09 124421 8

# HUTCHINSON

Peter Bucknall,
<u>Mackays of Chatham PLC</u>

5th December 1994

Dear Peter,

**<u>MUD,SONGS AND BLIGHTY</u>**

Can you please see whether any film for the above title formed part of the ex-Anchor Brendon shipment.If so,could you please let me have it back.

Best regards,

RANDOM HOUSE, 20 VAUXHALL BRIDGE ROAD, LONDON SW1V 2SA

TELEPHONE 071 973 9680  FAX 071 233 7870

RANDOM HOUSE UK LIMITED  REGISTERED No. 954009
REGISTERED ADDRESS 20 VAUXHALL BRIDGE ROAD  LONDON SW1V 2SA

# MUD, SONGS AND BLIGHTY

—A SCRAPBOOK OF THE FIRST WORLD WAR—

# Contents

# Acknowledgements

'Acknowledgements' is a poor word for expressing my gratitude to the many contributors who have helped me compile this book. In response to my appeals for information and personal anecdotes, I received such an immense amount of varied material that my most difficult task lay in deciding what I must leave out. I could only include material that related to the themes of the songs included in these pages: thus I was forced to omit many contributions that, because of their extraordinary interest, should and will be preserved for future use.

Special mention must be made of four contributors whose help was indispensable. Alfred Payne for an indomitable spirit, a wry humour and ability to boost a flagging morale: Violet Green whose husband, Tom, sadly died during preparation of this book: Percy Maggs for supplying me with a superb collection of Bamforth postcards: and M. V. Woodgate for extracts from her perceptive articles as a First War journalist.

In addition, I am indebted to the British Legion, the Imperial War Museum, the Illustrated London News, the BBC Music Library and the Central Music Library of Westminster for providing the facilities and information needed to obtain much of the material in this book.

Finally, I must acknowledge the courtesy of the many publishers, authors and individuals who have allowed me to reproduce extracts from previously published works, including illustrations, music, poetry and prose.

Every attempt has been made to obtain permission for all material used in this anthology. Some original sources have proved impossible to locate and I hope that I will be forgiven for any oversight on my part in not obtaining permission for such material.

My thanks are due to the following:—

C. W. Archer: L. Arnold: Ascheberg, Hopwood and Crew Limited for permission to reproduce 'Keep The Home Fires Burning' (Novello/Guilbert Ford): Beaverbrook Newspapers Ltd., Books Department for extracts from 'Songs That Won The War': Ernest Benn Ltd for 'Tipperary Days' by Robert Service: William Blackwood & Sons: The Bodley Head for poems by E. A. Mackintosh: Reuben Bray: BBC Music Library: The British Legion: Jean Armour Brown: RSM F. Buller-Thomas: Cambridge University Press for poems by Charles Sorley: Jonathon Cape Ltd for extracts from 'The Outlaws' by Ernst Von Salomon: Jonathon Cape Ltd and the Seven Pillars Trust for an extract from 'Seven Pillars of Wisdom' by T. E. Lawrence: Carroll Carstairs for an extract from 'A Generation Missing': V. Carter: Cassell & Co. Ltd for extracts from 'Vain Glory' by Guy Chapman: Chatto & Windus Ltd for an extract from 'Black Monastery' by A. Kunz, translated by Ralph Murray: Chatto & Windus Ltd and the Executors of the Estate of Harold Owen for poems from 'The Collected Poems of Wilfred Owen': H. S. Clapham: G. Clark: Catherine A. Cole: Constable & Company Ltd for 'Rendevouz' by Alan Seeger: Sidney Cox: Brooke Crutchley: Ernest Dickenson: J. W. Dobell: Gerald Duckworth & Co. Ltd for poems by Osbert Sitwell and T. M. Kettle and for an extract from 'Into the Blue' by Norman Macmillan: EMI for permission to reproduce 'I'll Make A Man of Everyone of You', 'Goodbye-ee', 'Tipperary', 'There's a Long Long Trail', 'Where Are the Lads In The Village Tonight?', 'Take Me Home To Dear Old Blighty', and 'The Laddies Who Fought And Won' (Francis, Day & Hunter Ltd & B. Feldman & Co. Ltd): H. N. Edwards: W. Fawkes: J. F. Gentry: Violet Green:

Wyn Griffith for an extract from 'This Not The Song They Wish to Hear': H.M. Stationery Office for extracts from Parliamentary Reports and the Official History of the War: Alf Holland: Reverend Geoff Holland: K. Howeld: Molly & Vic Howes: Lady Hulse for extracts from 'War Letters of Captain Sir Edward Hulse': Hutchinson Publishing Group Ltd for an extract from 'The Home Front' by Sylvia Pankhurst and an extract from 'Retreat from Death' by Herbert Hill: The Imperial War Museum: The Illustrated London News, Syndication & Archives Department for numerous extracts from The Graphic: R. G. A. Jakes: S. Kiek, Doran & Co. Ltd for an extract from 'A Tank Driver's Experience' by Arthur Jenkin: Colonel F. Lushington: Percy Maggs: The Machine Gun Corps Journal: Mr. & Mrs. H. J. Mitchley: R. H. Mottram for an extract from 'Three Personal Records': John Murray Publishers for a poem by W. N. Hodgson: E. T. Nettleingham's 'Tommy's Tunes': The New Statesman for a poem by Philip Johnstone: Mrs. D. M. Newton-Wood for an extract from W. S. Turner's 'Men of Death': Alfred A. Payne: Lt. Col. J. H. Plumridge, OBE: O. Devereux-Price: Punch: A. G. Reeve: R. W. Reeves: Richards Press for an extract from Patrick Miller's 'The Natural Man': G. T. Sassoon for the poems of Siegfried Sassoon: S. Shoop: E. W. Simon: Christopher South: Lady Spears for extracts from E. L. Spear's 'Liaison': G. E. Steele: D. Taylor: C. R. Tennant: Peter Tewson: Edward Thompson for an extract from 'These Men My Friends': G. Thorpe: P. Turrell: H. J. Vale: J. Vail, Machine Gun Corps: Westminster Central Music Library: L. P. Wilkinson: T. L. Wilson: Lt. Col. E. R. Winnall: H. A. Woodgate: M. V. Woodgate.

Did you have to fight the cockroaches, Nan?
And when they brought the telegram
Of John's heroic death at Mons,
Did you thank Lady Blair for the five shillings,
Making sure that the fender gleamed
Even as you cried your love goodbye?

Were those years hard, Nan?
The Roaring Twenties,
The Sighing Thirties,
You never said much;
Your kids enjoyed them
But then it was their youth
And they had to.
What was it for you, Nan?
Silent?
Lonely?
Perhaps better;
Perhaps he would have died in the kitchen,
Bellyful of beer -
But there was that job in the mill.

Did you cry in bed, Nan?
And did your hair,
Still long and soft and yellow when you held me,
Did it lie uncarressed across the pillow,
For the sixty years that left you,
With the memory of a shadow's embraces?

For what it's worth, I'll remember, Nan:
Remember those things you didn't tell me
And add them up;
And seeing that the total
Was gentleness and kindness,
Was trust and innocence,
Was loneliness and sacrifice,
Maybe, Nan, there was something in it,
After all.

*Colin Walsh*

# I'LL MAKE A MAN OF YOU.

Sung by

## MISS GWENDOLINE BROGDEN

IN

### ALFRED BUTT'S Successful Production

# THE PASSING SHOW.

(PALACE THEATRE, LONDON)

Book and Lyrics by

# ARTHUR WIMPERIS.

Music Composed and Arranged

by

# HERMAN FINCK.

COPYRIGHT.  PRICE 2/- NET.

LONDON:
FRANCIS, DAY & HUNTER,
138-140, CHARING CROSS ROAD. W. C.
NEW YORK:
T. B. HARMS & FRANCIS, DAY & HUNTER, INC., 62-64, WEST 45TH STREET.

*Copyright MCMXIV, in all Countries by Francis, Day & Hunter.*

# I'LL MAKE A MAN OF YOU.
## (Recruiting Song.)

Words by
**ARTHUR WIMPERIS.**

Music by
**HERMAN FINCK.**

**Tempo di Marcia.**

PIANO.

KEY E♭.

1. The ar—my and the na—vy need at—ten—tion,——— The out—look is—n't
2. I teach the ten—der—foot to face the pow—der——— That adds an ad—ded

health—y, you'll ad—mit,——— But I've got a per—fect dream of a new re—cruit—ing
lus—tre to my skin,——— And I show the raw re—cruit how to give a chaste sa—

For Permission to reproduce this publication on Mechanical Instruments written application must be made to Francis, Day & Hunter.

F. & D. 13419.

scheme, Which I real-ly think is ab-so-lute-ly it._____ If
lute, So when I'm pre-sent-ing arms he's fall-ing in._____ It

on-ly oth-er girls would do as I do I be-lieve that we could man-age it a-
makes you almost proud to be a wom-an When you make a strapping sol-dier of a

lone,_____ For I turn all suit-ors from me but the sail-or and the
kid,_____ And he says,"You put me thro' it and I did-n't want to

Tom-my I've an ar-my and a na-vy of my own._____ On
do it But you went and made me love you, so I did."_____ On

F. & D. 13419.

4

CHORUS.

Sun-day I walk out with a Sol - - dier, On
Sun-day I walk out with a Bo' - - sun, On

Mon-day I'm tak-en by a Tar, _____ On Tues-day I'm
Mon-day, a Ri-fle-man in green, _____ On Tues-day I

out with a ba-by Boy Scout, On Wednes-day, a Hus -
choose a "sub" in the "Blues," On Wednes-day, a Ma -

sar; _____ On Thurs-day I gang oot wi' a Scot -
rine; _____ On Thurs-day, a Ter - ri - er from Toot -

tie, On Friday, the Cap-tain of the crew; _____ But on
ing, On Friday, a Mid-ship-man or two, _____ But on

Sat-ur-day I'm wil-ling, if you'll on-ly take the shil-ling, To make a man of
Sat-ur-day I'm wil-ling, if you'll on-ly take the shil-ling, To make a man of

an-y one of you. On you. _____
an-y one of you. On you. _____

*ff*

*Fine.*

*f*

*D.C.*

F. & D. 13419.

Printed by HENDERSON & SPALDING, Ltd., Sylvan Grove, Old Kent Road, London. S.E.

8½A052814

IN concentrating on gigantic problems such as never before assailed a human brain, it is at least conceivable that "The Man at the Helm" should sometimes seek the soothing influence of **"My Lady Nicotine"**—perhaps **Craven "A."**

To the Kaiser, curse his sons,
Curse Von Tirpitz and the Huns,
Curse his blinkety, blankety guns—
    Curse him.

May his blood be sucked by chats,
Ticks and other vampires, bats,
And his earhole gnawed by rats—
    Curse him.

Freeze his nose and give him piles,
Stretch his lousy eyelids miles,
Rasp his legs with rusty files—
    Curse him.

May all his minions get like sap,
And all their noses run like a tap,
To blot them out from off the map—
    Curse 'em.

When filled up to his bleary eyes
The last vile sod a-dying lies
We'll wait until the —— dies,
Then o'er his grave these words inscribe—
    Curse him.
    Curse him.

# WAR DECLARED BY GERMANY.

### AMBASSADOR LEAVES RUSSIA.

## ULTIMATUM TO FRANCE.

### HOSTILITIES ALREADY BEGUN.

### LUXEMBURG INVADED.

### GRAVE BREACH OF TREATY GUARANTEES.

### BRITAIN INVOLVED.

## MEETING OF CABINET TO-DAY.

### ITALIAN ATTITUDE.

**"WE MUST KEEP OUT."**

**"REYNOLDS'S NEWSPAPER."**

What of the position of the United Kingdom? It can be stated in few words :—" We must keep out of it." In this land the voice of the mafficker is silent, and the whole people has its face set against war. . . . In such a time of stress and storm it behoves us to leave no stone unturned to make ourselves as ready as we can, so that if we are attacked we shall not be found wanting. Other nations also have put forth every nerve to get their armies and navies up to the best possible pitch. But whatever the outcome on the Continent, the duty of Great Britain is plain. No service to humanity will be rendered by our taking part in any war. The quarrel between Austria and Servia concerns us hardly in the remotest degree, and few Britons indeed would risk the life of a single soldier or sailor on one side or the other. . . . If we could become the decisive factor in the crushing of Germany and Austria it could but mean the aggrandizement of Russia. The Bear would become the dictator of Europe. Is that a prospect for which to send our men to death?

## SUNDAY SCHOOLS PRAY FOR PEACE

NEW YORK—Thirty million members of the World's Sunday School Association, scattered throughout the world, were to pray for peace Sunday.

The call for the peace prayer was issued by Sir Robert Laidlaw, president of the association, and is signed by him and by H. J. Heinze of Pittsburgh, E. K. Werner of this city, Frank L. Brown of New York, and the Rev. Carey Bonner of London.

## THE PATH OF HONOUR.

God of the people, King of Kings,
  Before whose secret purpose bow
The hopes of all created things,
  Oh, guard and guide our courage now!

Defend the right! No quest of gain,
  No thought of glory dims our eye:
For Peace we strove, we prayed—in vain!
  The blood of Europe makes reply.

The wealth, the blood to be outpoured,
  It is not that our hearts forget!
But honour, England's sacred word,
  We pray, is dearer to us yet.

Bring knowledge that not man alone
  But nations one day surely must
Give answer at Thy judgment throne
  As stewards of their earthly trust.

Let Peace still shine, a wistful star;
  In all the anguish make us one!
Guide us and guard us through the war
  We did not seek and could not shun!
              R. G. B.

## EMPEROR'S SPEECH.

### GREAT SACRIFICES REQUIRED.

#### GERMAN VERSION OF EVENTS.
#### A "STATE OF WAR."

BERLIN, Aug. 1.

Patriotic demonstrations in the Lustgarten outside the Imperial Palace continued all yesterday afternoon. At half-past six the German Emperor and Empress and Prince Adalbert appeared at the balcony of the Knight's Hall and received a great ovation. Amid bursts of thunderous cheers his Majesty spoke the following words :—

"A dark day has to-day broken over Germany. Envious persons are everywhere compelling us to defence. The sword is being forced into our hand. I hope that if at the last hour my efforts to bring our adversaries to see things in their proper light and to maintain peace do not succeed we shall with God's help wield the sword in such a way that we can sheathe it with honour.

"A war would require enormous sacrifices of blood and property from the German people, but we would show our adversaries what it means to attack Germany, and I now commend you to God. Go to church. Kneel down before God and ask him for help for our brave army."

Cries of "Hoch!" and "Hurrah!" and the singing of patriotic songs responded to his Majesty's address.

On their Majesties leaving the Palace soon afterwards in an open motor-car they once more received a tremendous ovation.

Oh, Mr. Lloyd George, have you got a shell,
Yes, sir, millions to blow the Huns to H——.
We'll stand no interference
Now that the end's in sight,
And dam and blast the neutrals,
That feel too proud to fight.

Humpty Kaiser sits on the wall,
Playing with soldiers and letting them fall,
But the Allies determined with money and men,
The Kaiser will never play soldiers again.
        (S'only a rumour.)

MR. LLOYD GEORGE

**THE TRUMPETER (1).**

Trumpeter, what are you sounding now?
Is it the call I'm seekin'?
"You'll know the call," said the Trumpeter tall,
"When my trumpet goes a speakin'
I'm rousin' 'em up, I'm wakin' 'em up,
The tents are astir in the valley,
And there's no more sleep with the sun's first peep,
For I'm sounding the old 'Reveille.'
Rise up!" said the Trumpeter tall.

BAMFORTH (Copyright).
WORDS BY PERMISSION OF MESSRS. BOOSEY & CO.

**MARIGOLD (1).**

Why are the boys dress'd in khaki to-day?
It's the war, Marigold, it's the war;
Why are they cheering and shouting hooray?
It's the war, Marigold, it's the war.
Don't let them see the tears falling like rain,
They're ready to fight for old England, that's plain,
They came back before, and they'll come back again
From the war, Marigold, from the war.

BY ARRANGEMENT WITH MESSRS. FRANCIS, DAY & HUNTER, THE PUBLISHERS OF THE MUSIC.
BAMFORTH COPYRIGHT.

### The Ragtime Soldier
Sung to the tune of "Ragtime Lover."

He's a ragtime soldier,
Ragtime soldier.
Early on parade every morning,
Standing to attention with his rifle in his hand
He's a ragtime soldier
As happy as the flowers in May
    (I don't think!)
Fighting for his King and his Country,
All for a shilling a day.

# A Call from the Trenches.

*(Extract from a letter from the Trenches.)*

"I SAW a recruiting advertisement in a paper the other day. I wonder if the men are responding properly —they would if they could see what the Germans have done in Belgium. And, after all, it's not so bad out here—cold sometimes, and the waiting gets on our nerves a bit, but we are happy and as fit as fiddles. I wonder if————has joined, he certainly ought to."

Does "————" refer to you?

If so

## ENLIST TO-DAY.

# God Save the King.

## Recruiting

'Lads, you're wanted, go and help,'
On the railway carriage wall
Stuck the poster, and I thought
Of the hands that penned the call.

Fat civilians wishing they
'Could go and fight the Hun.'
Can't you see them thanking God
That they're over forty-one?

Girls with feathers, vulgar songs –
Washy verse on England's need –
God – and don't we damned well know
How the message ought to read.

'Lads, you're wanted! over there,'
Shiver in the morning dew,
More poor devils like yourselves
Waiting to be killed by you.

Go and help to swell the names
In the casualty lists.
Help to make a column's stuff
For the blasted journalists.

Help to keep them nice and safe
From the wicked German foe.
Don't let him come over here!
'Lads, you're wanted – out you go.'

There's a better word than that,
Lads, and can't you hear it come
From a million men that call
You to share their martyrdom?

Leave the harlots still to sing
Comic songs about the Hun,
Leave the fat old men to say
Now *we've* got them on the run.

Better twenty honest years
Then their dull three score and ten.
Lads, you're wanted. Come and learn
To live and die with honest men.

You shall learn what men can do
If you will but pay the price,
Learn the gaiety and strength
In the gallant sacrifice.

Take your risk of life and death
Underneath the open sky.
Live clean or go out quick –
Lads, you're wanted. Come and die.

E. A. MACKINTOSH

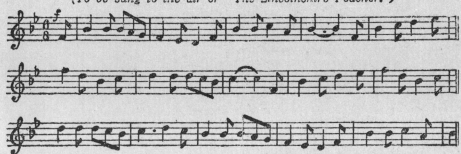

# THE GENTLE RECRUIT

*(To be sung to the air of "The Lincolnshire Poacher.")*

When war broke out with Germany I thought as I'd enlist.
"Old Uncle Joe can do my job" thinks I. "I won't be missed."
Now I'm the softest-hearted chap, I want to make that clear,
And I speak no ill of Kaiser Bill, *but I wish I had him here.*

I got inside a khaki suit and a soldier lad was I.
I'd lived a peaceful kind of life and I wouldn't hurt a fly,
But now my gun and cartridge clips to me are fond and dear.
And I speak no ill of Kaiser Bill, *but I wish I had him here.*

They shipped me off to Flanders though I'd never left dry ground.
That blooming ship went up and down and everything went round.
I shut my eyes and softly said, though feeling mortal queer—
"Oh, I speak no ill of Kaiser Bill, *but I wish I had him here.*"

They sent me to the trenches, and a lot of things I've seen.
I've had a bit of fighting, and I've done my fighting clean.
To do my duty civil like I always persevere,
And I speak no ill of Kaiser Bill, *but I wish I had him here.*

To love our fellow men, my lads, is what we all must do.
There's good in every one of us, and in the Germans too,
But the Huns that met my bayonet, they won't drink no more beer,
And I speak no ill of Kaiser Bill, *but I wish I had him here.*

JESSIE POPE.

# CAN YOU STILL HANG BACK? IT MAY BE **YOUR** SISTE

## GERMANY'S BLACK PAGE OF SHAME.

### Slaughter, Outrage, Pillage And Arson Shown In Official Report.

### NEITHER SEX NOR AGE SPARED.

### The Bavarians' Ferocity Against Hapless Civilians.

### 3,000 BELGIANS KILLED.

A terrible record of slaughter and outrage by the German troops in Northern France is revealed in an official report issued by the French Government yesterday—a black page in German history only equalled by that of the atrocities in Belgium.

Foremost among the troops who thus disgraced their name were the Bavarians, whose King in his birthday message issued this week talks of their ancient glory and renown and of their cultural development.

The Commission of Inquiry into German atrocities in Belgium reports on Province of Namur that of

### *Three Hundred Thousand Inhabitants*

the Germans have killed

### *Over Three Thousand.*

At Dinant alone seven hundred were killed, including seventy-one women and thirty-one children under fifteen years of age.

### KULTUR'S INDICTMENT.

Here are a few typical incidents from this volume of 20,000 words:—

German soldiers sought out people who were in their houses and shot them. In many cases they broke into houses and fired at everyone they saw.

A woman aged ninety-eight was bayoneted in bed and her body burnt in her burning house.

A boy of fourteen was disembowelled, and a lad of twelve, accompanying his father to pick potatoes outside a town, was shot with his father.

A harmless old man, aged seventy-eight, was brutally shot in the street on the pretext that he had shot some Germans, which was absolutely denied by his family.

### INHABITANTS SHOT LIKE RATS.

The frontier town of Nomeny, now a heap of charred ruins, was the scene of a massacre on August 21. The inhabitants were shot like rats in their houses or in the streets while trying to escape. The mayor was among the victims. The houses were pillaged and burnt.

In the cellar of a certain house several families, in all thirteen persons, had taken refuge. The Bavarians set fire to the house, and forced the unhappy people in the cellar to come out into the open, where they were shot down one by one. Among the killed were a boy of ten and a girl of three. A girl of seventeen escaped only by feigning death, and her baby sister was badly wounded in the elbow. Two women barely escaped with their lives after being severely wounded by bullets. The rest of the party, who were all men, were killed.

### THE DEVILRY OF THE BAVARIANS.

The report says that the greater part of the devilry in the Vosges seems to have been the work of Bavarians. In the presence of crime of this kind it is scarcely worth while to enumerate mere acts of pillage, although innumerable authenticated instances of such are recorded. It is noteworthy that the report, while it mentions the pillage of the chateau of the Baron de Baye, in the Marne, says nothing of the Crown Prince's presence there, although, according to the Baroness de Baye, the Prince stayed there and robbed the house himself.

The report states that the Baron's room, which had been sacked and the furniture broken, had been occupied by a person of high rank, as was shown by a chalk inscription indicating that it was reserved for a prince. A German general who stayed in a neighbouring house told his host that the Duke of Brunswick occupied the chateau.

### FATE OF WOMEN AND GIRLS.

The report mentions innumerable cases of the violation of women and girls. It is impossible to describe these abominations in detail; suffice it to say that elderly women and little girls were in numerous cases the victims of the brutal lust of the German soldiery.

At Montmirail an old man was shot for endeavouring to defend his daughter from a German

## THE BAVARIANS' CULTURAL DEVELOPMENT.

*With pride and joy I look upon the brave Bavarian army, which has confirmed its ancient renown and in glorious battles has proved itself a worthy member of the German army.*

*My confidence is immutable that the overwhelming defeat of our enemies will enable me to lead my people forward on the road to economical and cultural development.—Birthday message of King Ludwig of Bavaria to his people.*

*The greater part of the devilry in the Vosges seems to have been the work of Bavarians.*

*At Gerbeviller they proceeded to avenge their losses on the civil population. They burst into the houses, shooting, stabbing, and capturing the inhabitants—sparing neither age nor sex—and burning and sacking the houses.*

*A woman aged 78 was shot and her body afterwards shamefully profaned.—French official report on German atrocities.*

the muzzle of his revolver against her breast to enforce obedience.

One of the most terrible massacres in France was that at Gerbéviller, in the Vosges, on August 24.

Bavarian troops entered the town after having sustained heavy loss from a handful of chasseurs-a-pied, and proceeded to avenge themselves on the civil population. They burst into the houses, shooting, stabbing, and capturing the occupants—sparing neither sex nor age, and burning and sacking the houses. Over 100 persons disappeared, of whom at least half were massacred.

A woman aged 78 was shot, and her body afterwards shamefully profaned.

A man named Lingenhehd was shot, and while he was still living the Germans poured petrol over him and set fire to it in the presence of his mother.

Another man, the father of a family, was deliberately burnt alive in a barn.

Two young girls, who took refuge in a stable, were seen by the Bavarians, who followed them and shot at them. One was killed, but the other escaped.

A similar massacre seems to have been deliberately provoked by the Germans at Lunéville, as there had been no fighting there for some days previously. The Mayor, on August 25, saw German soldiers firing at the garret of a neighbouring house. The Germans declared that the inmates had fired at them.

### RABBI AND SISTER KILLED.

Among the "guilty" civilians was the Rabbi of the Jewish community, M. Weill, who was well known for his inoffensive character.

M. Weill and his sister (aged 16) were killed, and their house burnt.

Irritated, no doubt, by the remarks made by an officer to a soldier, against whom Mlle. Procés, a young girl of 19 years of age, had complained on account of his insulting proposals, they burned the village of Triancourt and organised a massacre of the inhabitants.

Fearing, not without reason, for their lives, Mlle. Procés, her mother, grandmother (71 years old), and an aunt (81 years old) endeavoured to climb from their garden into the next by means of a ladder. Only the young girl succeeded in escaping to the other side, and avoided death by hiding in a cabbage field. The three others were shot down.

On the following night the Germans played the piano amidst the corpses. When the Curé protested, the Duke of Wurtemberg replied, "What do you expect? Like you, we have bad soldiers."

At Chateau Thierry a girl of 14 was seized by three soldiers, two of whom outraged her. The third, touched by her entreaties, spared her.

### WHY COAL PRICES MAY SOON GO UP.

Although London coal prices have not advanced so far, a leading merchant stated yesterday that transport difficulties would undoubtedly force up prices in the near future. There is considerable congestion on the railways in consequence of shortage of labour and military requirements, and there is a very serious shortage of transport labour in London.

There is also a shortage of horses, and a lack of men at the pit owing to many enlistments. This has reduced the colliery output.

### FRANCE CALLING UP MORE MEN.

The *Echo de Paris* says:—"The Military Governor of Paris has just asked all the recruiting officers in his district to report to him on the condition of all exempted men and men of the auxiliary lines who are regarded as fit for service, but have not yet been enrolled.

"It is therefore probable that these men will shortly be given their marching orders, and similar steps will doubtless be taken in the provinces."—Reuter.

## PRIESTS TORTURED.

### Churches As Stables, Cures Flogged And Shot, And Bishops Ill-used.

The arrest of Cardinal Mercier appears to be but the climax to a policy of methodical mal-treatment of the Catholic clergy of Belgium pursued by the German invaders from the first.

At the request of the Belgian Legation in London the Press Bureau yesterday issued a list of specific instances of barbarous ill-treatment, of which evidence has been collected by the commission of inquiry.

Not only have churches and religious houses been destroyed or profaned in almost every village and in many towns through which the German Army passed, but in many places the sacred vessels were stolen when they had not previously been placed in safe concealment. Churches and religious buildings have even been utilised as stables or prisons.

#### HOISTED ON A CANNON.

There is, in particular, the case of the aged priest of Buechen, Father M. de Clerck, who on August 21 was arrested by German soldiers and accused of having fired at them. This was entirely false, for he was suffering from disease, and for some time had not even been able to conduct Divine service.

This poor invalid, 83 years of age, was hoisted on a cannon, then pulled down, and cast into a ditch.

**Next some soldiers took him by the arms and legs and dragged him along the pavement. The old man, tortured in this fashion and absolutely exhausted, said that he would rather suffer death than the continuance of such cruel treatment. He was then shot.**

#### VILLAGE PRIEST FLOGGED.

A priest, who escaped death by a miracle, makes this deposition:—

"On Tuesday, August 15th, at about 9 a.m., the Germans arrived in swarms at the village of Schaffen. Pretending that shots had been fired at them—which was wholly untrue, for no one had even thought of resistance—they began to murder, burn, and pillage. About 170 houses, including the town hall and the priest's house, were burnt to the ground; and 27 civilians (one of whom was the clerk) were murdered in cowardly fashion.

"Once they thrust me into the burgomaster's house, which was on fire, and then they dragged me out of it again. This treatment lasted the whole day. Towards evening they told me to look at the church, adding that it was the last time that I should set eyes on it. At about 8.45 they released me, after flogging me with a riding whip. I was bleeding badly, and lying on the earth, when an officer told me to get up and go off.

#### BISHOP WITHOUT A BLANKET.

The Bishop of Tournai, aged 74, was seized as a hostage, taken to Ath and treated with great rudeness. He had neither bed to lie on nor blanket to cover him, and one soldier struck him on the back with his fist. In the same diocese three ecclesiastics were shot, the curés of Roselies and Acz and a seminarist of Tournai.

# WHICH? WILL YOU BE
# A VOLUNTEER OR A CONSCRIPT

EXT

## To Germany

You are blind like us. Your hurt no man designed,
And no man claimed the conquest of your land.
But gropers both through fields of thought confined
We stumble and we do not understand.
You only saw your future bigly planned,
And we, the tapering paths of our own mind,
And in each other's dearest ways we stand,
And hiss and hate. And the blind fight the blind.

When it is peace, then we may view again
With new-won eyes each other's truer form
And wonder. Grown more loving-kind and warm
We'll grasp firm hands and laugh at the old pain,
When it is peace. But until peace, the storm
The darkness and the thunder and the rain.

C. H. SORLEY

WOMEN of BRITAIN SAY — "GO!"

For the Kaiser he started the whole bloomin' war,
So we'll strafe old Bill till he swanks no more,
And the King shall be boss where the Hun was before,
When we haul up the flag in the morning.

EASURING A MAN

Little French Baby,
The Bosch ain't no bon
Takin' your daddy —
Long years he's been gone.

Little French Baby,
Can't help feeling blue —
Guess it's because
I've a kiddy like you;
God grant I shall see him
Some day when we're through —
Little French Baby, bonjour napoo!

It had come at last! his own stupendous hour,
Long waited, dreaded, almost hoped-for too,
When all else seemed the foolery of power;
It had come at last! and suddenly the world
Was sharply cut in two. On one side lay
A golden, dreamy, peaceful afternoon,
And on the other, men gone mad with fear,
A hell of noise and darkness, a Last Day
Daily enacted. Now good-bye to one
And to the other . . . well, acceptance: that
At least he'd give; many had gone with joy:
He loathed it from his very inmost soul.

The golden world! It lay just over there,
Peacefully dreaming. In its clear bright depths
Friends moved – he saw them going here and there
Like thistledown above an August meadow:
Gently as in a gentle dream they moved,
Unagonized, unwrought, nor sad, nor proud,
Faces he loved to agony – and none
Could see, or know, or bid him well-adieu.
Blasphemous irony! To think how oft
On such a day a friend would hold his hand
Saying good-bye, though they would meet next day.
And now . . . He breathed his whole soul out,
Bidding it span the unbridged senseless miles
And glow about their thoughts in waves of love.

MAX PLOWMAN

## PRAYER FOR THOSE ON THE STAFF

Fighting in mud, we turn to Thee,
   In these dread times of battle, Lord,
To keep us safe, if so may be,
   From shrapnel, snipers, shell, and sword.

But not on us, for we are men
   Of meaner clay, who fight in clay,
But on the Staff, the Upper Ten,
   Depends the issue of the Day.

The staff is working with its brains,
   While we are sitting in the trench;
The Staff the universe ordains
   (Subject to Thee and General French).

God help the staff – especially
   The young ones, many of them sprung
From our high aristocracy;
   Their task is hard, and they are young.

*O Lord, who mad'st all things to be,
   And madest some things very good,
Please keep the extra A.D.C.
   From horrid scenes, and sight of blood.*

See that his eggs are newly laid,
   Not tinged as some of them – with green;
And let no nasty draughts invade
   The windows of his Limousine.

When he forgets to buy the bread,
   When there are no more minerals,
Preserve his smooth well-oiled head
   From wrath of caustic Generals.

*O Lord, who mad'st all things to be,
   And hatest nothing thou has made,
Please keep the extra A.D.C.
   Out of the sun and in the shade.*

*Julian Grenfell*

GENERAL JOFFRE

GENERAL HAIG

## From *How Shall we Rise to Greet the Dawn*

Continually they cackle thus,
   These venerable birds,
Crying, 'Those whom the Gods love
Die young'
Or something of that sort.

OSBERT SITWELL

FIELD-MARSHAL
LORD KITCHENER

TUNE: "*Your King and Country Need You.*"

For we don't want your loving,
And we think you're awfully slow
To see that we don't want you,
So, please, won't you go.
We don't like your sing-songs,
And we loathe your refrain,
So don't you dare to sing it
Near us again.

Now, we don't want to hurry you,
But it's time you ought to go ;
For your songs and your speeches
They bore us so.
Your coaxings and pettings
Drive us nigh insane :
Oh ! we hate you, and'll boo you and hiss you
If you sing it again.

The world bloodily-minded,
 The Church dead or polluted,
The blind leading the blinded,
 And the deaf dragging the muted.

*Israel Zangwill*

### I DON'T WANT TO BE A SOLDIER.

TUNE: "*Come, my lad, and be a Soldier.*"

I don't want to be a soldier,
I don't want to go to war ;
 I'd rather roam
 Here at home,
And keep myself on the earnings of a lady typist.
I don't want a bayonet in my stomach,
Nor my eyelids shot away,
 For I am quite happy
 With my mammy and my pappy—
So I wouldn't be a soldier any day.

### ONWARD, QUEEN VICTORIAS !

TUNE: "*Onward, Christian Soldiers.*"

Onward ! Queen Victorias,
Guarding the railway line.
Is this " foreign service " ?
Ain't it jolly fine ?
No ! we're not downhearted.
Won't the Huns look sick ?
When they meet us over there,
All looking span and spick ?
Hope on, Queen Victorias !
Don't forget the fray.
We shall do our duty
For a bob a day.

### WHY DID WE JOIN THE ARMY ?

TUNE: "*Here's to the Maiden of Sweet Seventeen*"
 *and "Fol-the-Rol-Lol."*

Why did we join the Army, boys ?
Why did we join the Army ?
Why did we come to Salisbury Plain ?—
We must have been ruddy well balmy.
 Fol-the-rol-lol, fol-the-rol-lol,
 Fol-the-rol-lol, me laddie ;
 Fol-the-rol-lol, fol-the-rol-lol,
 Fol-the-rol-lol, me laddie.

The blackbird sings to him, 'Brother, brother,
 If this be the last song you shall sing,
Sing well, for you may not sing another;
 Brother, sing'.

SIR JOHN FRENCH

*Julian Grenfell*

21

# A RUMOUR ABROAD

It's 1914, as I strolled around the Chin-ming Market in Peking, fascinated by the activity of the centipedes moving in and out of a heap of sugared peanuts on a stall. Rumours and counter-rumours of War were all over the British Legation; the War was supposed to be between France and Germany. Nobody paid much attention at the time and life went on as usual.

To be stationed in Peking, North China, what was it all about and what were we there for? Kitchener once said and I quote:- 'If anything happened to our troops in the Far East, all we could do was to build a memorial to their memory', and thanking God for those few kind words, which cheered me up no end at the time. Of course we were only youngsters and didn't care much, but after 50 years I sit and wonder what it was all for.

My memory goes back to the last public execution on the International Bridge in Tientsin when a string of poor devils knelt there and a bloke in a long white robe appeared with a long sword, held them by the pigtails and chopped off their heads. It was just another Chinese custom to me then, but a nightmare when I think back. But who was I to complain, I was just a seven bob a week  private soldier serving in His Majesty's Army.

*from Tom Green's Journal*

Abie, Abie, Abie, my boy,
What are we waiting for now?
You promised to marry me
Sometime in June.
It's now December,
And I'm like a big balloon.
Abie, Abie, Abie, my boy
What are we waiting for now?

SO YOU WANT TO BE A SOLDIER, LITTLE MAN! (4).

Little Man! Little Man! playing on your drum, rat-a-plan,
 You are mother's only son, never mind about a gun!
Stay at home! stay at home! fight for her and love her
 all you can,
 You are mother's only son, never mind about a gun!
 Little Man! Little Man!

BAMFORTH (Copyright).
COPYRIGHT: ASCHERBERG, HOPWOOD & CREW. LTD., 1911.

**THE SOLDIER'S GOOD-BYE (1).**

I'm now under orders, my darling, I'm going away
 to the war,
And to-day is our last day together, we've never
 been parted before.
Let us go just across the old meadow where first
 we made love, you and I,
And tell me once more that you love me, and kiss
 me and bid me good-bye.

BAMFORTH (COPYRIGHT).        WORDS BY KIND PERMISSION OF MESSRS. BOOSEY & CO.

## TAKING SIDES

Anyhow, back to the Legation and the rumours, we learned early one morning that the French had marched round to the German Legation only to find it completely empty, the Germans had scarpered to a fortress named "Sing-Tow". This place was supposed to be well fortified with enough provisions to last seven years. The "South Wales Borderers" were sent there eventually and my lot was all bustle packing up, and all large cases being marked "Silcot India". Things were exciting now, everybody wondering whether we should be home in time for France before the war was over, for we discovered that destination "Silcot India" was only a blind for leaving the country. We were not to leave so soon however and I found myself on guard next day, the guard room being just inside the Civil Legation Gate.

*from Tom Green's Journal*

---

### List to the Call

Written by a little Australian girl, aged 11.

*The blare of trumpets, the rush of feet,*
*As they marched away down Macquarie Street.*
*They were gay, and laughing, and merry then,*
*But, oh! will they ever come back again?*

*They drilled 'neath Egypt's burning sun,*
*And forth they went to meet the Hun;*
*For men must fight for honour's sake,*
*Tho' tears may fall, and hearts may break.*

*They sailed past Lemnos Island fair*
*To fight for the land they held so dear.*
*Who has forgotten the charge by the deep*
*Under the shadow of Gaba Tepe?*

*" Killed in Action," so some of them fell,*
*Fighting away in that grim hot hell,*
*Or " died of wounds " 'neath that scorching sun,*
*Or " wounded " or " missing," their duty done.*

*Thro' the streets come the wounded men,*
*Heroes all of them, home again.*
*Australians, attention! List to the call,*
*They are blowing the trumpets, crying for all.*

*Go, men! fight for the Southern Cross.*
*Stand by it! Fall for it! gain or loss.*
*You men, you shirkers, do not lag,*
*Fight for Australia, the King and the Flag.*

WINSOME JENNINGS.

## RECRUITING SONG R.F.C. No. 1.
### Special Tune.

I was standing at the corner,
When I heard somebody say :
" Come to join the Flying Corps,
Come, step along, this way."
I threw my thirty  chest out,
And put my cap on straight,
And walked into the office
Along with Jack, my mate.

They offered me two bob a day,
I said, " I didn't think,"
But when they murmured, " Four bob,"
I said, " Come, have a drink."
And now I spend my Sundays
With Lizzie in the Lane.
I wonder when I'll get my " first "
Or see an aeroplane.

I never was so well off
In all my naturel :
You should see me in St. James's,
I am an awful swell.
And now I've been to Larkhill,
My education is complete.
" Form fours," " 'Bout turn," " Two deep,"
Oh ! don't I do it neat.

You should see us hold our heads up
When the others pass us by.
The girls they all run after us
And, breathless, say, " Oh my !
Dear Tommy brave, I'll be your slave,
If you will take me up."
But hastily I answer,
" I've an invitation out to sup."

## JOBS FOR THE BOYS

The  majority grasp little beyond the fact that their husbands have got work, and they have good money coming in. And if the worst does happen, they will be quite practical and stoical, the elementary nature after all does not hold much capacity for suffering. But a few will mind, and they will mind in a dumb, desperate way which the neighbours will not understand. They will find no comfort—at least not at first—in the dramatic touch their position holds. Theirs will be that grief which makes those who look at it feel dumb, and all words seem inadequate and awkward. *'Seul le silence est grand: le reste est faiblesse.'*

In the East End all "the adventures of peace, adventures of the mind and spirit," are unknown, or almost so. To a few the war is a very big thing. Reservists' wives understand a little what it means; but the greater number, as I have said, are untouched by it still. The men themselves, when they went to enlist, went because they were "out of a job." In no case that I have met did they go from sense of patriotism. But in their letters is a suggestion of it, revealing itself in a complete absence of complaint, in delight in their little sham fights, in their longing to get to the Front. There is nothing *blasé* in these letters. The enthusiasm is great, even if it does not go much further than intense personal delight in a new uniform. There in camp at Aldershot, at Sheerness, they are living, really living. From the East End, Mons and the Aisne somehow do not seem so terrible. If they have brought death, they have also brought life.

*M. V. Woodgate: The English Churchwoman*

## Arm-chair

If I were now of handsome middle-age,
I should not govern yet, but still should hope
To help the prosecution of this war.
I'd talk and eat (though not eat wheaten bread),
I'd send my sons, if old enough, to France,
Or help to do my share in other ways.

All through the long spring evenings, when the sun
Pursued its primrose path toward the hills,
If fine, I'd plant potatoes on the lawn;
If wet, write anxious letters to the Press.
I'd give up wine and spirits, and with pride
Refuse to eat meat more than once a day,
And seek to rob the workers of their beer.
The only way to win a hard-fought war
Is to annoy the people in small ways,
Bully or patronize them, as you will!
I'd teach poor mothers, who have seven sons
– All fighting men of clean and sober life –
How to look after babies and to cook;
Teach them to save their money and invest;
Not to bring children up in luxury
– But do without a nursemaid in the house!

If I were old or only seventy,
Then should I be a great man in his prime.
I should rule army corps; at my command
Men would rise up, salute me, and attack
– And die. Or I might also govern men
By making speeches with my toothless jaws,
Constant in chatter, until men should say,
'One grand old man is still worth half his pay!'
That day, I'd send my grandsons out to France
– And wish I'd got ten other ones to send
(One cannot sacrifice too much, I'd say).
Then would I make a noble, toothless speech,
And all the list'ning Parliament would cheer.
'We cannot and we will not end this war
Till all the younger men with martial mien
Have enter'd capitals; never make peace
Till they are cripples, on one leg, or dead!'
Then would the Bishops go nigh mad with joy,

Cantuar, Ebor, and the other ones,
Be overwhelmed with pious ecstasy
In thanking Him we'd got a Christian,
An Englishman, still worth his salt, to talk.
In every pulpit would they preach and prance;
And our great Church would work, as heretofore,
To bring this poor old nation to its knees.
Then we'd forbid all liberty, and make
Free speech a relic of our impious past;
And when this war is finished, when the world
Is torn and bleeding, cut and bruised to death,
Then I'd pronounce my peace terms – to the poor!

But as it is, I am not ninety yet,
And so must pay my reverence to these men –
These grand old men, who still can see and talk,
Who sacrifice each other's sons each day.
O Lord! let me be ninety yet, I pray.
Methuselah was quite a youngster when
*He* died. Now, vainly weeping, we should say:
'Another great man perished in his prime!'
O let me govern, Lord, at ninety-nine!

OSBERT SITWELL

SWEARING IN MEN AT SOUTHWARK (under Major Jackson, of Polar fame)

POLICEWOMEN: BEFORE AND AFTER GOING INTO UNIFORM

THE FARM-HAND
in her rustic apron.

A "FARMER'S BOY"
in the old-time smock.

TO THE
YOUNG WOMEN
OF LONDON

Is your "Best Boy" wearing Khaki? If not don't YOU THINK he should be?

If he does not think that you and your country are worth fighting for—do you think he is WORTHY of you?

Don't pity the girl who is alone—her young man is probably a soldier—fighting for her and her country—and for YOU.

If your young man neglects his duty to his King and Country, the time may come when he will NEGLECT YOU.

Think it over—then ask him to

JOIN THE ARMY TO-DAY

THESE WOMEN ARE
DOING THEIR BIT

LEARN TO
MAKE
MUNITIONS

WOMEN'S LAND SERVICE CORPS

I LEAVE
THE LAND TO
YOU

WANTED 5000 EDUCATED WOMEN BETWEEN 18 & 35 FOR WAR WORK ON THE LAND

The office boy is no more. The creature of many duties and vast potentialities (for there never was a millionaire yet who did not begin his financial career as an office boy) has been promoted to fresh fields. Peace be unto the ashes of his career! It is more glorious in these days to be the least and latest of our Tommies than to be a millionaire in the making. And meanwhile the office girl replaces him. A smart young person in an overall may be entrusted almost everywhere with your important message; and the chances are that she will deliver it with greater promptness, and with a sterner sense of duty, than our late friend of the peppermint bull's-eyes and penny dreadfuls. Her new responsibilities weigh heavily upon her, for she is inaugurating a new era of feminine labour. Perhaps an office girl or two, a few female ticket-collectors and a postwoman here and there do not warrant this pomposity of language. They are the swallows which promise, but do not make, the summer of the new era, and at present their popularity in the illustrated Press is against them. When surprised and snapshotted at their labours they wear the self-conscious smirk of the photographed celebrity, and not a line in their faces and figures hints at any absorbed interest in their task. But the absorbed interest is there, and the outward and visible sign of this inward and spiritual grace, seldom possessed by the " young lady " typists of other days, is an overall. It is the distinguishing mark of the new era.

The great things in life seem to spring from trifles, and the connection between the two is mysteriously hidden. Hence the relation of overalls to new eras must be seen as yet with the eye of faith. To any other eye the overall is a sensible covering worn by the new office girl for no other purpose than to keep her clothes unspotted from the dust and ink of offices. But if it were so really, why did not the lady typist adopt it? She, it seems to me, was prevented from doing anything so sensible by the " lady " qualification which she never managed to outgrow. In the dark ages of fifteen or twenty years ago, when first she sprang herself upon us—greatly to her credit, for pioneering, even on a typewriter, is weary work—the bloom had not yet been rubbed off her ladyhood. She worked at the office from ten to six, but from six to ten she was the young lady at home, anxious to live down the day's experiences. Office work was a thing to be got through as soon as possible, and to be finally forgotten in a grand *dénouement* of white satin and orange blossom.

In the course of years, other young ladies, not ladyfied at all, modelled themselves religiously upon her pattern. Flimsy and diaphanous of blouse, to the limits of decency and beyond them, gay with hair ribbons and gorgeous in incredible pearl earrings and pendants *à la Nouveauté de Paris*, they looked the part, certainly to their own, if to no one else's, satisfaction. The costume typified their mental attitude towards their work. It alone, and the world which it stood for, mattered. And so work came to be divided into work, and women's work. Male and female created He them, and male and female too was the corresponding reward of their labours. If the just suffered with the unjust, the conscientious with the frivolous, the sensible of dress with the preposterously attired, it was nobody's fault. The standard was one of sex, not of merit.

As a sign of the new era of feminine labour the overall is not impressive, but this very lack of pomp and ceremony is a point in its favour. It is a uniform. Everybody knows how men and women in uniform become imbued with a sense of the responsibility, the honour, and the moral strength of the cause which their uniform stands for—qualities which, as mere persons in mufti, they would not possess. Any lapse is a disgrace to the uniform, and, therefore, to the cause which it represents. But these noble qualities do not make for individual inspiration, and *esprit de corps* in most cases degenerates into *esprit d'uniforme*. This is the case in Germany. With us the man is the uniform, plus his character. Imperial Government does not encourage character, and if a man, in spite of orders, shows any signs of it, it has no use for his talents. To make up, it gives him the finest gold lacings, the tightest trousers and most gaudy coats in the world. The more splendid the uniform, the less, you may depend on it, there is behind it. How much does a profession owe to its uniform? It is not only picturesqueness that suffers when the old, appropriate dresses are forgotten. Farming paid in the days of smocks, and although the farmer's present troubles may be due to foreign importation, still his neglect of the smock, that should have been his trade mark and his pride, showed a lack of interest which is the first step to failure. Is the adoption of a uniform of labour, therefore, the first step to success? I think so. It argues a new attitude towards the work. It proves that women are ready to sink their vanity, and that work, henceforth, will be work, without qualification of sex.            CANDIDA.

AN "OFFICE GIRL"
in her dainty overall.

A LOCK-KEEPER
in jersey and top-boots.

## The Woman's Part

*They would not have us weep. . . .*
  *Dear boys of ours, whom we have lost awhile;*
*Rather they'd have us keep*
  *Brave looks, and lips that tremble to a smile.*
*They would not have us grieve—*
  *Dear boys of ours, whose valiant hearts are*
    *stilled;*
*Nor would they have us leave*
  *Our task undone, our service unfulfilled.*

*They would not have us mourn. . . .*
  *Dear boys of ours, who leapt to that clear call;*
*And though our hearts are torn,*
  *The heaven-sent hope is ours: " Death is*
    *not all! "*
*Almost we hear you now—*
  *Dear boys of ours, who marched to Freedom's*
    *goal—*
*" Set firm hands to the plough,*
  *And guard our honour safe in England's soul! "*
        HELEN SEVREZ.

## WARMING UP

It was lovely to be back in blighty. The ship was being unloaded. The married quarters was the problem, some had been married, mostly in Malta, before going to China and had no proper homes; women and children were crying as the men said their goodbyes, fell in and marched off. To crown it all the sea water had got into the baggage hold and most of the women's clothing was ruined, poor devils. I don't know how they got on, whether any claim was made or not.

I was detailed to stay with the women and children until their train arrived. They were given tea and refreshments. At last the train arrived and all were safely packed in and they waved to me with tears streaming down their faces.

"Destination"? Depot. Bristol. I eventually arrived at the camp to join the regiment "Mournhill Camp", Winchester and blimey was it cold, mud

and under canvas, we were dished out with eight lengths of overcoat material for blankets, 22 in a tent, one had to take his tunic off to let his mate get by. It was murder, bags of excitement drawing different kit, woollen scarves, leather jerkins, fur coats from god knows what animals and who the hell was going to carry all this, I thought, as I gazed at the heap on the floor and the bugle still sounding to come and sign for some more. This went on for a few days, then the word "leave", which had been on our minds came really into action. Three bloody days embarkation leave; some had to travel up north, some had been abroad several years. We were told off in pairs, queer arrangement, I thought. I was paired off with a chap from Hoxton, London. I remember his words well – you go first Tom as I shall not be back in three days, neither was he. I went home for three days. I lived at Paddington, wasn't long enough to see everybody, but I went back to time. The idea of the pairs was if one chap from the first batch was a day over his leave, his partner lost that day from his leave. I thought this was real daft. Send to Horfield Barracks if you like and get it confirmed, as I have already said every word is true.

*from Tom Green's Journal*

AN APPEAL TO YOU

INVASION OF ENGLAND

Bill and will went up the Hill Just to Pick some Fruit

They both came down with a terrible frown. assisted by John Bull's Boot.

# WAR
## TO ARMS CITIZENS OF THE EMPIRE!!

IF IT'S A GERMAN—GUNS UP!

TUNE: *" If It's a Lady—Thumbs Up!"*

If it's a German—Guns Up!
If it's a German with hands up,
Don't start taking prisoners now,
Give it 'em in the neck and say " Bow-wow."
If it's a German—Guns Up!
Stick him in the leg—it is sublime.
If he whispers in your ear,
" Kamerad! Kamerad!"
Guns Up—every time.

Wish I were 40 again!

*Through Darkness to Light* **THE ONLY ROAD FOR AN ENGLISHMAN** *Through Fighting to Triumph*

HERBERT CHAPPELL.          July, 1917.

MILITARY TAILOR & BREECHES MAKER.

Partners (HERBERT A. CHAPPELL          50, Gresham Street,
          (JAMES A. CHAPPELL                    London, E.C.
                              LONDON WALL 7264.

CLOSE AT 1 p.m. ON SATURDAY.          TERMS NET CASH.

### OFFICERS SERVICE OUTFIT.

| | | |
|---|---|---|
| Khaki Whipcord, Barathea, or Serge Service & R.F.C. Tunics from | £3. 15. 0. | |
| " " " " Knicker Breeches " | 1. 12. 6 | |
| " " " " Slacks ... " | 1. 7. 0 | |
| Bedford Cord Infantry Breeches ... ... " | 2. 5. 0 | |
| " " Cavalry Breeches (Strapped buckskin) from | 2. 15. 0 | |
| Khaki British Warm, fleece lined & complete with stars " | 3. 15. 0 | |
| Burberry Infantry Raincoats ... ... ... | 3. 13. 6 | |
| " Cavalry " ... ... ... | 4. 4. 0 | |
| Cording's Raincoats (rubber) ... ... ... from | 4. 10. 0 | |
| Khaki Service Cap (badges extra) ... ... from | 12. 6 | |
| "Sam Browne" belt complete ... ... ... | 2. 5. 0 | |
| Best Flannel Shirt ... ... ... | 10. 6 | |
| Khaki Silk Tie ... ... ... | 2. 6 | |
| Folding Sleeping Bags ... ... ... | 3. 0. 0 | |
| Wolseley Valise ... ... ... | 3. 7. 6 | |
| Valise & Camp Kit inclusive ... ... ... £7. 15. 0 & 3. 15. 0 | | |

Regimental Jumpers, Mess Jackets & Overalls to order.

Haversacks, Mess Tins, Water-bottles etc.

Regimental buttons and badges extra.

### INDIAN & EGYPTIAN OUTFITS.

| | | |
|---|---|---|
| Trench Coats ... ... ... ... from | 4. 10. 0 | |
| Fleece Undercoats ... ... ... " | 1. 15. 0 | |

*Francis, Day & Hunter*
REGᵈ Nº 257,748. *Sixpence Nett*

**Nº 1506 SIXPENNY POPULAR EDITION. (NO DISCOUNT ALLOWED)**

*The Weekly Dispatch (with every good reason)*
*Proclaims it in headline "The Catch of the Season."*

# "Good-Bye-Ee!"

*Written and Composed*
*by*
*R. P. Weston and Bert Lee.*

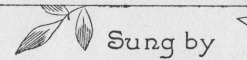

Sung by

# MISS DAISY WOOD

# MISS FLORRIE FORDE

AND

# CHAS. WHITTLE.

FRANCIS, DAY & HUNTER.
(PUBLISHERS OF SMALLWOOD'S PIANO TUTOR)
138-140, Charing Cross Road, London, W.C.2.

NEW YORK: T. B. HARMS & FRANCIS, DAY & HUNTER, INC., 62-64, WEST 45ᵗʰ STREET.
SYDNEY: J. ALBERT & SON 137-139, KING STREET.

Copyright 1917, by Francis, Day & Hunter.

# "GOOD -BYE - EE !"

Written and Composed by

R. P. WESTON & BERT LEE

PIANO

1. Bro - ther Ber - tie went a
2. Mar - ma-duke Ho - ra - tio
3. At a con - cert down at
4. Lit - tle Pri - vate Pa - trick

-way    To do his bit the oth - er day _____ With a
Flynn,    Although he'd whis - kers round his chin, _____ In a
Kew    Some con - va - les - cents dress'd in blue _____ Had to
Shaw    He was a pri - son - er of war _____ Till a

## GOOD-BYE, DOLLY GRAY! (1).

I have come to say good-bye, Dolly Gray!
It's no use to ask me why, Dolly Gray!
There's a murmur in the air, you can hear it ev'rywhere,
It is time to do and dare, Dolly Gray:
Don't you hear the tramp of feet, Dolly Gray,
Sounding through the village street, Dolly Gray?
'Tis the tramp of soldiers' feet, in their uniforms so neat,
So good-bye until we meet, Dolly Gray!

## HOW CAN I BEAR TO LEAVE THEE ? (1)
### (Soldier's Farewell).

How can I bear to leave thee ?
One parting kiss I give thee :
And then whate'er befalls me,
I go where honour calls me.
  Farewell, farewell my own true love.
  Farewell, farewell my own true love.

## ANGUS MACDONALD (1).

O sad were the homes in the mountain and glen,
When Angus Macdonald marched off with his men;
O sad was my heart when we sobbed our good-bye,
And he marched to the battle, maybe to die.

## WHEN THE FIELDS ARE WHITE WITH DAISIES. (1).

I stood once in a harbour as a ship was going out,
  On a voyage to a port beyond the sea.
And I watched a blue-clad sailor as he said his last farewell
  To the lassie who loved him most tenderly.
I saw the teardrops falling as the last Good-bye was said,
  T was the sorrow of a parting all must learn.
And I heard the sailor promise to the lassie now in tears:
  "When the fields are white with daisies I'll return."

## Good-bye

Parody. Composed and sung by R. Walker (Decoys).

I HEARD a funny song one day,
Sung in a very sloppy way ;
But as it went so fine,
I wrote this one of mine.
If it is not sense it's gay.
For to shove this song I've sighed,
Every publisher I've tried,
And to our O.C. I shouted out with glee,
Just read this ! He did, then he cried—

### Chorus

Ay, ayee ; ay, ayee,
Goodness knows, to compose, you've had a try-ee,
To a D.C.M. you'll go,
You'll be sentenced to death I know ;
Don't cry-ee ; don't sigh-ee,
There's still a chance you will not have to die-ee ;
Swing the lead, see the Doc,
Say you've got shell-shock,
C'est la guerre ; your "ticket's" there,
Good-bye-ee.

The Sergeant-Major read it too,
He said, " Of songs I've seen a few,
As you've worked so hard, do an extra guard,
Then perhaps a fatigue or two."
This made me feel so sick and sad,
I next pulled up a small French lad,
I says, " Look, garçon, compris this new song ? "
He looked at it, then yelled like mad—

### Chorus

Good-bye-ee, good-bye-ee,
Confiture, cigarette, bread pour moi-ee,
Plenty hitchy-koo, no bon,
Damn, blast, bully beef, carry on,
Jamais cry-ee, jamais sigh-ee,
Beaucoup (boko) Anglais soldats toujours cry-ee,
Cheerio, Mam'selle, compris go to ——,
Merci bien, parti vite,
Good-bye-ee.

When the moon shines bright on Charlie Chaplin,
He's going balmy
To join the Army ;
And his old baggy trousers want a-mending
Before they send him
To the Dardanelles.

sLO·O·OPe

# FOLLOW THE DRUM

## THERE MUST BE NO MORE STRIKES IN WAR-TIME.

### By HORATIO BOTTOMLEY (Editor of "John Bull").

With stern and resolute determination, but at the same time with throbbing and earnest sympathy, Mr. Bottomley—hardest of "workers" himself—talks to the men on whom our Army depends for a speedy and decisive triumph in the West, telling them that in the present condition of affairs no strike is in any circumstances justifiable, and imploring them to be not less self-sacrificing and enduring than their brothers in the trenches and on the sea.

I REJOICE to know that the engineers' strike has at last been settled, but all the same I want to-day to have a very solemn talk with the men who have been "out"—talk of man to man—brother to brother—aye, and may not I say, worker to worker? I really don't think anyone works harder than do I. I am *always* working—even at my play. And although I am not a duly accredited Labour Leader, the man for whom I work hardest, and love to work for, is the Man in the Street—a phrase which connotes all the toilers of the nation, and all the sailors and the soldiers—God bless them. I am "with them" all the time.

\* \* \* \*

And to-day I have something to say to them—as I had to the Clyde workers two years ago, when, with the approval of the present Prime Minister, I called them together and had a heart-to-heart chat with them. Later I spoke to the Miners and the Railwaymen—and in each case was accorded that sympathetic attention which only full mutual trust could engender. For I do not mince my words. Flattering, humbugging and pandering to the masses is not leading them—it is *following* them; and that, in my view, is where so many of the professional leaders go wrong. Try to put yourself in their place and to appreciate the circumstances of a dispute as they affect *them*, and if you have any claim at all to offer advice they will listen to you—*so long as you speak in language they can understand*.

\* \* \* \*

So come, boys, let us have a confab. I don't even now know exactly what the row has been about; but I am going to assume that you were in the right—that either private employer or Government controller was largely to blame. But do you know that out there in the trenches—where your boy, or your brother, is—they, too, are having a devil of a time? All sorts of real, grim grievances, believe me; but not a word of complaint escapes their lips, whilst as to striking—well, you know what that would mean. Now I want you to bear this fact in mind all the time I am speaking to you.

## A CATCHWORD OF HISTORY.

"The Times" chose a good moment last week to reprint the full text of the Kaiser's order to his troops at Aix la Chapelle before the battles of Mons and Cambrai. We reminded our readers even then that the idea of annihilating any British troops who dared to land upon the Continent was a fixed mania with the War Lord of innumerable spiked helmets. The mania published itself in these words:—

"It is my Royal and Imperial command that you concentrate your energies, for the immediate present, upon one single purpose, and that is that you address all your skill and all the valour of my soldiers to exterminate first the treacherous English and to walk over General French's contemptible little Army."

This ignoble and impotent effusion has proved to be about as unhappy an utterance as was ever linked with an Imperial name. It will furnish one of the catchwords of history. Nothing more was needed to show the Kaiser to be a pinchbeck paladin without true chivalry of soul. It was the outburst of a vulgar Emperor.

## "THE ETERNAL GOAL."

### TO THE EDITOR OF THE TIMES.

Sir,—In connexion with a letter headed "The Eternal Goal" in your issue of April 8, may I add the following episode? A few days ago I visited an encampment of Sikhs, with whom I conversed with the help of an interpreter. On leaving them I said, "You worship the one God, do you not?" "Yes," was the reply. I then said:—"He is the same God as our God. May He bless and guard you as well as us." As the interpreter communicated this message to them their faces kindled and a low murmur of satisfaction ran through the group; and as I turned to ride away they lifted up a strange cry, rising high and sinking low, of salutation and farewell.

I remain yours faithfully,
April 10.        CHAPLAIN AT THE FRONT.

## ROOM FOR EVERY MAN IN NEW ARMY.

### Lord Kitchener Does Not Think Number of Men Coming Forward Will Be Sufficient.

### GREAT LOSSES, BUT SLIGHT COMPARED WITH FOE'S.

### Our Troops Are in Excellent Spirits and Confident of Success.

Lord Kitchener, in the House of Lords yesterday, said he did not think the number of men coming forward would be sufficient. He thought the time would come when they would require many more.

In reply to Lord Curzon, who asked as to the numbers of recruits, Lord Kitchener said: "We have nothing to complain of. We are getting, approximately, 30,000 per week, besides regiments formed locally."

As regards numbers, there was room for every man who is ready to come forward and serve his country, and he was sure that all calls which were made on the manhood of the nation would be promptly responded to.

Our troops are in excellent spirits, he said, and are confident of success.

Our losses have been great, but slight as compared with those inflicted on the enemy.

**LORD KITCHENER:**

"The British Empire is now fighting for its existence."

"I have no complaint whatever to make about the response to my appeals for men."

"But I shall want more men, and still more, until the enemy is crushed."

"Besides the troops from the Dominions there are now training in this country over a million and a quarter of men."

"The men at the front are doing splendidly."

"We may confidently rely on the ultimate success of the Allies in the western theatre of the war."

**MR. ASQUITH:**

"Belgium must be restored and recompensed."

"France must be established within her original boundaries."

"The safety of the little nations must be secured for ever."

"Prussian militarism must be utterly crushed."

"To this end all classes of our people, rich and poor, high and low, must be prepared to make personal sacrifices."

**MR. CHURCHILL:**

"The Navy, in spite of losses, was relatively and actually stronger at every point than our enemies' navies."

"Six or nine or twelve months' hence they would see results, silently achieved, which spelled the doom of Germany."

# EVERY MOTHER'S SON IS READY TO CARRY A GUN

## N.C.Os BY ONE WHO ISN'T

N.C.Os receive higher rates of pay than us, to enable us to do their work. They have always existed in the army, and we suppose they always will. At one time, they were one of us, but when decorated tape appears on one of their sleeves, they are certainly one of 'them'. They are generally up to the standard of men in the ranks, sometimes beneath the standard, but they all have louder voices. The louder their voices, the quicker the promotion. Some swear at you, and some don't, but I expect they know all the recognised words. They can be thoroughly relied upon to nose out all the best billets but should we, by hard work, make our billet comfortable and attractive, they immediately relieve us of any further responsibility in the building. They are invariably smartly dressed, which possibly explains the deficiency in the supply of clothing.

What they do in their spare time is a mystery. We have our ideas but would rather not express them in writing. There are two classes of N.C.Os - technical and non-technical. The former are better paid, and are responsible for rendering all motor transport unserviceable. By so doing, they do good to their country by creating industry. The non-technical supervise us, putting things right. This is a very good system because it ensures everybody being employed. As a body they are extremely useful for consuming canteen wet goods and introducing you to the O.C. or C.O. in the event of you doing something out of the ordinary. No N.C.O. has ever been seen to lift a gas tube, but they are all qualified and extremely willing to teach us how to. There is only one case on record of an N.C.O. lifting a gas tube, but he died shortly after and the custom has not been encouraged.

They are not anxious to be demobilised, as they realise that they have good jobs. They are even signing on for another three years! The rumour that some of them may work after the war is **not** founded on fact.

*The Balloon Times*

PRIVATE JACK HORNER went in the corner,
Eating " Machonichie " stew,
He said with a frown,
As he chucked the tin down,
" When the H—— is a roast about due ? "

OLD Major Hubbard went to the cupboard
Of souvenirs he'd quite a few,
But a Mills' bomb in there
Went off with a glare,
And now the poor Major's napoo.   (R.I.P.)

# NORTH LONDON IN WARTIME

In behind the Angel, just midway between it and King's Cross station, there is a network of little streets where many soldiers' wives and mothers live. They are richer than their sisters of the East-end, but such riches have not brought them respectability - rather the reverse - and they are less naive, have less of the child about them, are more suspicious. For nobody cares much about Islington. The East-end and South London have each their own distinctive personality, but North London is vague, indeterminate, colourless. Yet to those who know it, even very slightly, it has a certain interest all its own.

There is one street which is grander than any other in the quarter. The principal church stands in it, so does the vicarage, and the houses that occupy each side of it are tall and grey and sombre.

Four separate families, all of whom I know quite well, live in one of them. With those who rent the ground floor I should by rights have no dealings, for their only link to the war is that of dwindling trade, which they lay to its account. I cannot fancy, however, that even in times of profoundest peace, their trade was ever a thriving one. They are doll makers. The man is old, with a long, grey beard and tall, thin figure, that lend him an air of strange dignity, and he talks in a way that suggests some education. No one wants to buy dolls now, he tells me - at least, not such as he makes. People only like cheap toy dolls, whose original came from Germany. In olden days it was different, in Victorian days children only had one doll, but it was very good, and they cherished it accordingly. And he has clung to those Victorian times, and decorates his little window with big staring waxen images, whose long, uncurled wigs are labelled "real hair", and whose lowest price is 7s. 6d. From the barrows round the corner you can buy them fashionably dressed, and their wigs curled, all for 6d. Those barrows are always crowded, but no one ever enters the old man's shop, where he sits alone hour after hour adding to the stock of which nobody wants to buy. It was he who first told me of the family which occupies the topmost floor.

'There's another soldiers wife up there, miss, that you never go to see,' he told me, so one day I climbed the uncarpeted wooden stairs, and found up there a young wounded artilleryman and his still younger wife. She is just twenty-one, but she has often talked to me since of things she used to do when 'she was a girl'. Her husband is just twenty-four, but he looks older, for he is ill, though suffering as much from rheumatism contracted in the trenches as from wounds. He was in the retreat from Mons - the trenches were nothing to that and he knew both.

'They're great soldiers, miss, the Germans. They were round our flank once. If they'd know the little lot of us there was, they could have smashed us clean. But they didn't know. There's such a lot of spies with the French, young fellers, soldiers in the regiments. I saw once an old farm woman arrested - leading her cows about she was. Whichever way she turned 'em was signal to the enemy. Sounds strange, miss, but it's true. The Belgians is fine soldiers.'

He is curiously unboastful, and I have never heard the history of anything he has done. He doesn't mind if he does have to return to the front.

While he talks, and he talks well, his little wife sits on a stool before the stove, rocking the baby in her arms, and listening to him with a curious smiling wonder difficult to convey. Once, when he was not there, she showed me his picture in a STAR of last November. He was one of a group of "Cheery Wounded Heroes". Her hand shook a little as she pointed him out to me, and she became very breathless as she told me how he got his wound.

The wives of two other soldiers live on the floor below, but the artilleryman's little wife does not know them: she says she does not mix much with other people. One of them is a little deaf; she has no children; and her husband is in Kitchener's Army. I have seen her often, in afternoon as well as morning, but I have never seen her without a row of curling pins fastened tightly to her head. Presumably they remain there night and day throughout the week, and are taken out just for Sunday afternoon. To the mere outsider it is a question of whether the game is worth the candle.

The wife of a man in the Army Service 'Corpse' stationed at 'Ruin' is next door to her. She is a sad little thing, devoted to her husband and greatly oppressed by the war. She is longing for him to get leave and come home, but at the same time dreads the thought of once more parting from him. He writes to her often, and has sent her Princess Mary's gift to himself - the pipe, packet of tobacco and cigarettes, and Christmas card, together with the card of the King and Queen. She wants to have them all framed together, but the frame would have to be in the nature of a case, and that would cost too much. She keeps all his letters and picture postcards, and gloats over them when she is alone. She says time hangs so heavy without him, for when she has done all her cleaning there is nothing left to do; the children are at school all day. But I think she would miss her grief were she to be without it. She always ignores any suggestion for the obtaining of more work, and to take any but a gloomy view of the war distresses her.

In another street, which is quite close, though not so grand, one of those women who the War Office describes as an "unmarried wife" lives. I once suggested to her that she should marry the man with whom she had lived for the last twelve years, but her eyes flashed at the mere idea, and she said she would rather commit suicide at once. I have heard since that he drank, and ill-treated her, and I fancy the ill-treatment

**FAREWELL, ISABELLE (1).**

Hark the drums, how they beat, Isabelle,
To the tramping of feet, Isabelle,
So dry your eyes, sweetheart, don't cry,
Wish me good luck and say good-bye.
There is work to be done, Isabelle,
There's a fight to be won, Isabelle,
Into line I'll fall—when the bugles call
Hurry up! come along! come along! Bamforth (Copyright).
WORDS BY PERMISSION OF THE LAWRENCE WRIGHT MUSIC CO., 8, DENMARK ST., W.C.

**FAREWELL, ISABELLE (2).**

Farewell, Isabelle, Isabelle, don't let it grieve you—I've got to go!
Farewell, Isabelle, Isabelle, I've got to leave you to face the foe;
You know very well, Isabelle, as the battle I go through,
I shall do my best when I'm in it to win it as I won you.
Bamforth (Copyright).
WORDS BY PERMISSION OF THE LAWRENCE WRIGHT MUSIC CO., 8, DENMARK ST., W.C.

must have been real, for these women seldom speak against their men folk; they excuse them rather than the reverse. This man is training in Ireland, and at Christmas time he got a few days' leave. Going away, he grew a little tearful, and said that perhaps he might never come back, that he might be killed in France; but she only replied that she hoped he might die a better man than he had lived!

Again, as in the East-end, there is amongst all the men a tremendous keenness, evidenced by their letters, or by the occasional glimpses one gets of them themselves. It is natural they should be keen, and also happy - keenness is in the air - and even if they never get to the front, still, dressed in their khaki, they are heroes in their homes if nowhere else. Their outlook has also become wider, their eyes a little opened.

'My son's at Bedfors, miss' a woman said to me the other day. 'Yes, miss, 'e's billeted there, at a lady's, miss, a real lady's, and 'e's picked up all 'er ways. Talks of 'serviettes' now 'e do, miss, and wears a mackintosh.' The last point seemed an odd one.

The change that has come over this part of London since the war first began is hardly noticeable. The women were never much interested in the events in France, and they are little more so now. They hate the Kaiser. Beyond that, however, they have no theories regarding the great struggle. But whereas in August and September the men were chiefly enlisting because they were 'out of a job' they are joining now from fear of a forced conscription. ' 'E thought he'd better go before 'e was made.' And the women part from them without any fears. The inadequacy of their own separation allowances, or the mistakes of the pay-masters touch them far more nearly than any thought of possible final parting from men, whose lives until now have been so singularly uneventful.

Just as in August and September, so now the majority do not take the war with any seriousness, and it is perhaps small wonder that they do not.

Last November I heard from a wounded private that the men in the trenches were betting peace would be signed by Christmas. Last week another told me the whole struggle would be over by July. The few who read papers find them equally optim-istic. So they are all happy about the future, and in the streets you hear the "Marseillaise" being sung, and the Russian National Anthem whistled, the latter as though it was something very bright and gay. And the men swagger about in khaki, and have their photographs done on postcards; and soldiers have become the centre of everything, and every-where there is an extra stir and life. It is all like a big game, a peculiar game, a little bit mysterious, but rather nice and quite exciting.

At times one wonders if it will be a game always, if a great awakening will ever come. Doubtless it will to the men going out so gaily to meet that greatest of all Great Adventures. But to those who are left behind? It is a question. Certain it is, however, that if it has all meant nothing to them, they in some vague, incommunicable way will be the poorer.

*M. V. Woodgate,*
*The Queen, The Lady's Newspaper*
*April 8, 1915*

But men have died to give them place
and they who live will one day sing
as I, will speak their sorrow once again,
but some will hear with sound a song
to lead the children into love
        Whose children these?
        Not theirs who died.

O Mercy give us grace to live
O God send wisdom soon.

       WYN GRIFFITH
    *from* **The Song is Theirs**

*"Dear Father,*  *"August 19th, near Louvain.*

"No writer can describe a battle, and he who says that he does not feel nervous when ordered to charge, bra

"After Tirlemont and Louvain, we scattered and rode precipitately here and there trying to reach Brussels. I w joined by three Belgians of the line, curiously enough, mounted. We chummed up at once, and, as our horses were qu done up, we decided to dismount and rest. We got through a thick high hedge, which separated the road from a l meadow, and squatted down, after fastening our horses to a tree ; but we were soon disturbed by a patrol of Uhlans, u passed us, singing loud, without, fortunately, seeing us. After some rest, and whilst discussing on our next move, noticed a faint light down the vale, a quarter of a mile off. We immediately made for this light. We arrived at house, front door opened, windows shattered, roof nearly off ; no one to be seen. We went in the cave [cellar], a there found what is hardly believable. Three creatures, one partially dressed, dead, and leaning against the wall, a a child clinging to her, and another young woman quite unconscious ; bottles of wine, empty, all over the place ; bro tables and chairs. We were debating what to do for the little child when we were surprised by the entry of two Germa Then began a strife impossible to describe. The intruders were overcome and killed ; but the horror, when we calmed do a bit, to find the child's head beaten to a pulp and the second woman dead ! We covered the poor creatures as well we could, and decided to have a rest for part of the night. We found plenty of bread, dry fish, pickles, bottles beer, and tallow candles. We lit another candle, and, taking from my knapsack this bit of paper and my indispensa bottle of ink, I squatted down and took a record of the horrid scene which I had just witnessed. Don't be too severe on artistic attempts ; I am out of it. It is as I saw it, bar that the first woman was almost naked. My comrades will f their way to Antwerp or [name of place unreadable]. If so, this letter will be handed to Edward, who will t it, as communications between Antwerp, or Ostend, and London are still open. I must find my way to Brusse God help me !

"PHILIP ROSSI."

---

*Stripping your neighbours is only to take away from them the means of doing you a mischief.*—FREDERICK THE GREAT.

*Above all, you must inflict on the inhabitants of invaded towns the maximum of suffering. . . . You must leave the people through whom you march nothing but their eyes to weep with.*—BISMARCK.

*The only means of preventing surprise attacks from the civil population [of Belgium] has been to interfere with unrelenting severity, and to create examples which by their frightfulness would be a warning to the whole country.*—THE KAISER.

*This war must be conducted as ruthlessly as possible, since only then, in addition to the material danger, is the necessary terror spread.*—GENERAL VON BERNHARDI.

*You cannot wage war with sentimentality. The more unmerciful the conduct of the war, the more merciful it is in reality, for the war is thereby sooner ended.*—FIELD-MARSHAL VON HINDENBURG.

*Inexorability and seemingly hideous callousness are among the attributes necessary to him who would achieve great things in war.*—FIELD-MARSHAL VON DER GOLTZ.

*The innocent must suffer with the guilty. All that is as nothing compared with the life of a single German soldier.*—GEN. VON BISSING.

*International law is by no means opposed to the exploitation of the crimes of third parties (assassination, incendiarism, robbery and the like) to the prejudice of the enemy. . . . The necessary aim of war gives the belligerent the right and imposes upon him, according to circumstances, the duty not to let slip the important, it may be decisive, advantages to be gained by such means.*—THE GERMAN WAR BOOK.

## Condemned out of Their Own Mouths

"It was to the discipline, rather than the want of discipline, in the German army that these outrages, which we are obliged to describe as systematic, were due," says the Report of Lord Bryce's Committee on alleged German outrages, and it will be seen from the above table that frightfulness has been approved and advocated by Germany's War-Lords and leaders.

The French view of the situation is characteristically summed up by M. Anatole France in his contribution to the inspiring "Book of France," just issued by Macmillan at 5s.: "The Germans have robbed the profession of arms of every vestige of humanity. They murdered peace ; now they are murdering war. They have made out of it a monstrosity too evil to survive."

---

## GOOD RIDDANCE

At Liverpool-street Station one day, amidst a crowd of weeping women watching husbands, sons, and lovers go off on a journey which for som would be so long, stood a woman who was not weeping. This was told to me by the women who had been there.

'We couldn't help but laugh, miss, even though we were both crying awful. She pushed 'er 'usban into the carriage, miss, and banged the door on 'ir and at the top of her voice she cries "Thank Gawc 'e's gone—thank Gawd 'e's gone.' We did laugh, miss.'

*M. V. Woodgate*

Good-bye to the family at Waterloo yesterday.

**"Aus großer Zeit."**

You will we hate with a lasting hate,
We will never forgo our hate,
Hate by water and hate by land,
Hate of the head and hate of the hand,
Hate of the hammer and hate of the crown,
Hate of seventy millions choking down,
We love as one, we hate as one,
We have one foe, and one alone—
England!

## The Hymn of Hate: or, The Teuton in his Tantrums.

In Quires and Places where they sing,
The Germans make the rafters ring,
Throughout the cultured Vaterland,
With Hymns of Hate, by high command.
A rage that's impotent, of envy born,
We greet with laughter—and a touch of scorn.

List to their crazy chorus: " Woe
To England, she's our only foe ! "
Alas, they likewise vilipend
The Turk, who is their only friend.
" This noble, deep and patient land " (Carlyle)
Appears to have a bad attack of bile.

" God punish England ! " is their cry
Directed to the Throne on High,
An order, mark you, not a prayer,
Sure symptom of a " crise de nerfs."
Thank Heaven, to Germans we are not germane,
No hate-wave melts the ice of our disdain.

W. K. C.

## A STRAFE ON THE KAISER.
### TUNE : Special.

We haven't seen the Kaiser for a hell of a time,
    Hell of a time—Hell of a time.
We came to France to see what he was doing,
The Royal Flying Corps will be his ruddy ruin :
Oh, we haven't seen the Kaiser for a hell of a time.
He must have been a-blown up by a mine.
Or he's the leader of the German band.
Gott strafe him, he's a cousin of mine.

## THE MOUNTAINS OF MORNE.
### (ANOTHER MOAN.)

Dear, mother I'm writing this letter you see ;
I'm a second A.M. in the R.F.C.,
And when I enlisted, a pilot to be ;
But oh ! 'tis never a bit of the flying I see.
The sergeant-majors, they bawl and they shout,
They don't never know what they're talking about.
Now if things don't alter I'll blooming soon be
Where the Mountains of Morne sweep down by the sea.

43

## OFF!

At last all leave finished, kit inspection almost every day. It appeared in orders that the following day there should be a "route march" and details of what kit to carry. This included ground sheet, leather Jerkin, the fur coat, etc., etc., labels were issued to be tied to spare kit bag containing our other kit. We then fell in for our "route march" but we never saw "Mournhill Camp" again. We were marched to Southampton and straight on the boat for France, that was our lot. I remember climbing the gang plank and dumping rifle and pack on deck and flopped on a coil of rope and watched the horses being pulled aboard in slings by crane, poor things, they were scared stiff. We stayed in port until it got dark. Suddenly the engines started up and we were off. The Divisional Commander had visited us at our messes on the boat and asked if we were comfortable. There was too much din and noise to hear replies from the troops. I expect his personal appearance was as welcome as a mother-in-law on her daughter's honeymoon, but I suppose he meant well. On landing in France and being met with a guide and several with hurricane lamps, we fell in and after roll call on the quay, we started marching, but blimey there is a certain "hill" in France I shall remember as long as I live. I knew when I had reached the top, my body appeared to straighten up, what a marvellous feeling. We had not far to go before we could get the load off our backs. Not much happened for the next couple of days, except some clot had an idea we were not making the weight and they dished us out with fifty rounds of ammunition.

*from Tom Green's Journal*

We are the Ragtime Army,
The Artists' O.T.C.
We cannot drill, we cannot shoot,
What earthly use are we ?
And when we've got to Berlin
The Kaiser he will say :
" Hoch ! Hoch ! mein Gott !
What a damned fine lot
Are the Artists' O.T.C."

"C"

## Where to Live—[ADVT.]

IN ONE OF THE CHOICEST LOCALITIES OF NORTHERN FRANCE.

TO BE LET (three minutes from German trenches), this attractive and WELL-BUILT DUG-OUT, containing one reception-kitchen-bedroom and UP-TO-DATE FUNK HOLE (4ft. by 3ft.), all modern inconveniences, including gas and water. This desirable Residence stands one foot above water level, commanding an excellent view of the enemy trenches.

EXCELLENT SHOOTING (SNIPE AND DUCK).

—Particulars of the Tenant, Room 6, Base Hospital, Boulogne.

## First Lesson in Elementary French for G. L.

(Have you saluted the sister of my gardener, by numbers?)

### I

*Souvent* means *Often*,
    *Me souvient*
Means *We remember*
    Where we were sent
For communication drilling,
At a shrunken daily shilling,
With a Church parade on Sunday,
And a route march every Monday.
*Souvent me souvient, si je puis,*
Rear rank steady—dress up number three.

### II

*Voulez-vous* is *Will you*,
    *Promenader*
Means—but you remember,
    Remember HER,
Girl you left behind you,
Demoiselles might blind you;
There's a Church parade on Sunday,
There's the front line on the Monday.
*Souvent me souvient, si je puis,*
Lady Margaret, pray for me,
Donna Margareta.

### III

*Si je* is *If I*,
    *Pu-is* is *Can*:
Say No Surrender.
    As you were, Man;
Pull yourself together.  Billing
    Isn't in our shrunken shilling,
And the girl you left behind you
    Walks alone upon your Oneday,
Weak and faithful, sad and kind, you
    Know; Remember This is Monday.
Sunday midnight.  We remember,
As we water some last ember
On our hearth, we will remember
(Advent comes in drear December)
How you sang and passed away,
While we watched and prayed for Day.
    Here we safely—thank you—stay:
    Here we—thank you—work and play.
*Souvent me souvient, si je puis,*
*Voulez-vous?...Je suis homme je fuis.*
*Depuis si longtemps moi j'y suis.*

J. H. A. HART.

INOCULATION

Jack and Bill went down the hill,
To play at " Crown and Anchor,"
M.P. came round and pinched their crown,
And C.B. followed after.

" By Goom! this jam do get in yer ears!"
(91ᵗʰ Manchester's)

## "IF" with apologies to Rudyard

If you can take a strafing on parade,
    Without an answer back.
If you can do your drill,
    And never smartness lack.
If you can learn,
    From one who knows no more than you,
And in your turn
    Make others do so too.
If you can keep your head
    When all about you,
Are losing theirs, and blaming it on you.
If you can prove, to officers who doubt you,
That you know something of platoon drill too.
If you can place your left foot sideways smartly,
    Bend your arms, and do not move your head.
Then stretch them forwards, upwards, sideways,
    Until with stretching you are fairly fed.
If you can down upon your hands
    And raising your legs alternately try to bite the grass.
Then up again upon your feet,
    And neither look nor feel a silly ass.
If when you wear your "Glad Rags"
    You do so in the regulation way,
And not indulge in slacks upturned,
    For that's a serious error of the day.
If you take heaps of notes and read them often,
    Gaining some knowledge of the arts of war,
And put your back into your work—
    A thing you may have never done before.
If you can shirk
    But not be found out shirking;
Or, if you must work,
    Work hard and stick to working,
You need not be afraid of R.T.U.
    They can't afford to lose such men as you.

# THE CALL TO COLOUR
## ON THE
# WESTERN FRONT

THE BLACK "BOYS" ARE NOW IN FRANCE HELPING TO
WIN THE WAR AGAINST A BLACKER FORCE THAN THEY

CHINESE VISITORS TO OUR FRONT IN FRANCE

Official photograph

It is particularly appropriate that China should break with Germany, for, alone of all nations, she has been consistently anti-militarist throughout the ages. She was also the first civilised country to taste German "frightfulness," when, during the Boxer rising, the Kaiser's troops spread the terror of the German name among the Chinese.

## SOMEWHERE IN FRANCE

I am sitting by the fireside as the evening shadows
Gazing idly at the pipe-rack, hanging sideways on
wall;
Underneath it in the corner, I can see an empty ch
And a pair of well-worn slippers that are waiting f
you there:
They remind me that across the seas you've gone,
And I am left alone to carry on:—

Somewhere in France, Somewhere in France,
Yonder across the sea;
While I am here fondly dreaming of you,
There you are dreaming of me:
For you will know where'er you go,
My heart is faithful and true;
Though you're far, far away
Every hour of the day
I am somewhere in France with you.

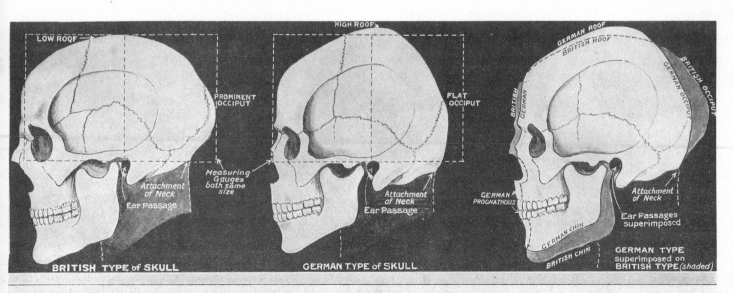

LONG-HEAD VERSUS SHORT-HEAD: OPPOSITE TYPES OF HUMANITY WHICH ARE FIGHTING FOR OPPOSITE IDEALS

A CONCISE GLOSSARY OF WORDS
AND PHRASES IN COMMON USE IN
HIS MAJESTY'S OVERSEAS FORCES

By B. H. and A. C.

Not joint authors of the King's English
or the Concise Oxford Dictionary

*Aussie.* Our comrades of the Kangaroo Feathers. They'll do us, digger.

*Bière.* Just Beer.

*Bock.* Ditto, plus gas, plus six sous.

*Bière Anglaise.* So called because it is brewed in France.

*Blighty.* A modern Utopia dreamed of by everyone on Service in France. Some authorities say it is a figment of the brain of some genius on the General Staff; in no way related to the *Utopia* of Sir Thomas More or Frank Morton.

*Billy doo.* The note you promise to write to Marie, but never do.

*Bully Beef. Compree?* See McConachie's.

*Censor, The.* A curious person, unknown, mysterious, and unfathomable, whose ways are not the ways of the common man; who knows no rules save those which his own moods or eccentricities dictate. He is a law unto himself—a rare Caligraphist, an ardent reader, the delight of the War-Office, the despair of the soldier, the civilian, and the journalist. God bless him—Perhaps!!

*Champagne.* A curious concoction (possibly made from stale rum, fixed bayonets, grenadine, and the River Lys); much in evidence on pay nights. The first portion of this word (English meaning) describes the beverage, the latter half describes the next morning.

*Débit de boissons.* Any hut, house, estaminet, barn, farm, or building, of, it matters not what size, description or degree of cleanliness where one can obtain drinks of various descriptions, and of varying degrees of vileness.

*De oofs.* Not related in any way to the pedal appendages of the equine species; a generic term for a kind of food much in favour at officers' messes. Cassell's dictionary spells it œufs. We are led to believe the translation is eggs.

*Eggsanships.* The Q.M.'s salvation.

*Encore.* (1) Fill 'em up again. (2) 'Savenother.

*Fine Beer.* A phrase which has the power to damp the ardour and depress the spirits of all troops. A synonym for this, is, Nahpoo booze. Translated, this means, "Sorry, gentlemen, we have no more liquor."

*Huit heures Monsieur.* A polite way of telling you that you have had your last drink for the evening.

*McConachie's.* Oh Hell!!!

## NIGHT TIME AT CAMBRIDGE.

Lieut. Bo-Peep used to walk in his sleep,
His batman sometimes couldn't find him,
One night he dam well met a Mademoiselle
He had left his pyjamas behind him.

10.14 P.M.

10.15 P.M.

10.17½ P.M.

**M.O.** That wise and mysterious person who listens to your inmost thoughts through a rubber tube, then listens sympathetically to your tale of woe, and then with a fiendish grin writes—No. 9, M. and D.

**Merci.** In French—Thank you. This should not be confused with the "Mercy Kamerad" of Fritz who is *not* thanking you in anticipation of a bayonet thrust. Here it means "Blease don'd."

**No Compree.** A diplomatic expression used by the natives of France, when they consider it advisable, not to understand your advances, whether spoken in *French* or *English*.

**Out of the Line.** A Euphemism for fatigue or working parties, to carry rations, sand-bags, etc., to dig saps, build up trenches, go out wiring, and do all sorts of work, necessary or unnecessary at any old hour.

**Pork and Cheese.** Army Anglo-French for Portuguese.

**Peut-être !** Variously interpreted. (1) You've got Buckley's chance. (2) I don't think. It does not refer to the staple food of Ireland or to Lord Rhondda's nightmare.

**Pork and Beans.** A malignant disease to which troops are constantly liable. Quartermasters are immune from it, but are frequently "carriers."

**Rest billets.** Headquarters Divisional fatigue and recruit-drill office.

**Rien à faire.** Not in these — circumstances. The usual reply to the soldier's question "Promenade ce soir?"

**Slack.** Nether garments issued by the authorities, to hide the "splendid" physique of the H'Anzacs.

**Saluting.** A most necessary practice for the winning of the war. For further particulars see our volume, The third NZ (R) Brigade (Publishers—Full Tunn and Co).

**Trays beans.** A phrase used for describing the Madamoiselle at your billet.

**Tout-de-suite.** This is, madam assures you, how she will attend to your order for vin blanc, but is not quite how you would describe, in pure colonial, her subsequent movements.

**Trenches.** Large well-built ditches (purely imaginary), usually detected by small (very) pieces of sand-bags, and duckboards.

**Verre.** A receptacle for beer.

**Vin blanc.** Pronounced variously, as, vang blong, vinn blanck, or vin the blonk. The despair of the analytical chemist.

**Zig zag.** An exhilarating condition arrived at by 8 p.m. daily, which inspired the author of that well-known song, "Follow the Tram-tracks."

B. H. AND A. C.

---

TUNE: "*There is a Happy Land.*"

Where are our uniforms?
Far, far away.
When will our rifles come?
P'raps, pr'aps some day.
And you bet we shan't be long
Before we're fit and strong,
You'll hear us say, " *Oui, oui, tres bong,*"
When we're far away.

---

**FRED KARNO'S ARMY**

An Inventions Committee was set up by GHQ in 1915 to consider ways of ending the stalemate of trench-warfare It tried out a giant fire-hose that would wash the Germans out of their trenches. Another idea was a sort of crocodile made of steel that would worm its way through the enemy wire; and a battery that would fire cables with grapnels to haul it out of the way. There was a projector-drum that would propel streams of hand-grenades into the enemy line, each fuze to be ignited by friction as the missiles emerged.

---

COAL FATIGUE.

TUNE: "*Here we are, Here we are, Here we are again.*"

Coal Fatigue, Coal Fatigue, Coal Fatigue again.
Forty tons of coal to be shifted a day

(Gawd blimey !)

Get your pick and shovel; do it at the double;
Are we downhearted ?—no; let it all come.
Coal Fatigue, Coal Fatigue, Coal Fatigue again,
It'd be enough to kill Kaiser Bill.
For if you get your dinner, it's a cert you are a winner,
So Coal, Coal, Coal Fatigue again.

Coal fatigue in a big camp during winter is a very distasteful job, especially in the mud of Salisbury Plain or the Curragh.

## AN ENGLISHMAN NEEDS TIME

*27th Aug. Hardecourt.* My impressions of the
English. Those I've seen (a) at Bray, a little incongruous. Some in caps, others in helmets. And the
helmet, down to their noses. Horsement who race.
Otherwise, good material. (b) At Hardecourt. A
Major with ribbons, very polite. In general, calmness
and indifference. Value of their artillery, one to three
of ours. But they shoot 'regardless'. At Falfemont
on the 24th, they broke down. Why? They said;
stopped by machine-gun fire. The fact remains, they
failed. Their faults: they look on war as a sport. Too
much calmness which leads to a 'go-to-hell' attitude.
A gunner subaltern at Hardecourt came up to see
where Combles lay! No consistency in their work.
They attack in and out of season, break down when
they ought to go through; and with a certain
spiritual strength, say: 'Oh, well, failed to-day; it'll
be all right tomorrow.' Nevertheless, there are still
so many shells wasted and so many men lost. To
sum it up, they still lack savoir-faire.

*Louis Mairet*

THE SOLDIER'S GOOD-BYE (2).

Be a true soldier's wife, bonnie darling,
For the fondest of hearts must part;
Tho' the soldier may tramp to the end of
the world,
His home is his true love's heart.

BAMFORTH (COPYRIGHT). WORDS BY KIND PERMISSION OF MESSRS. BOOSEY & C

GOOD-BYE, DOLLY GRAY! (2).

Good-bye, Dolly, I must leave you, though it breaks my hea
to go,
Something tells me I am needed at the front to fight the fo
See, the soldier-boys are marching, and I can no longer stay,
Hark! I hear the bugle calling! Good-bye, Dolly Gray!

BAMFORTH (COPYRIGHT). WORDS BY KIND PERMISSION OF CHAS. SHEARD &

39 last birthday & sound as a Bell.

# Ten Commandments Revised for Cadets.

## (VIDE ARMY ORDER, MARCH, 1917.)

I.  Thou shalt have no other caps but those properly wired.

II.  Thou shalt not take unto thyself any buff coloured ts, ties or collars, or any raiment of a similar gaudy hue, I, thy superior officer, am a very jealous "god," visiting the uity of such gay apparel on my junior cavaliers.

III.  Thou shalt not omit the salute to an officer ; for the , will not hold him guiltless that looketh into a shop window dopteth some other device to avoid this necessary observance.

IV.  Remember thy hat band to keep it white : on thy button ipment, boots, face, and thy jolly old musket shalt thou our and do all that thou hast to do, but thy hatband is the ticular pride of thy C.O. ; wherefore C2 it.

V.  Honour thy captain and thy "superior" officers that days may be long in the 2nd Officer Cadet Battalion, without of being ignominiously returned to thy unit.

VI.  Thou shalt not smoke a pipe in public places.

VII.  Thou shalt not commit defaultery.

VIII.  Thou shalt not parade thine imaginary ailments before M. O. on Gogs days.

IX.  Thou shalt not bear thy gas helmet with thee to rch and to lectures, but on all other parades.

X.  Thou shalt not covet thy lover's arm to be seen walking n in arm with her in public places: thou shalt not covet:—— NSORED! (Ed.)

REGINALD P. BATTY.

THE SOLDIER'S GOOD-BYE (3).

You'll think of me marching and fighting, away, far away over
    the sea ;
You'll keep a bright home for me, darling, and a place in your
    bosom for me ;
And if I must fall, bonnie darling, 'tis all that a soldier can do,
And the loyal old country I die for, will not be forgetful of you.

BAMFORTH (COPYRIGHT).        WORDS BY KIND PERMISSION OF MESSRS. BOOSEY & CO.

## OUR ESSEX CAMP.

TUNE : "Back Home in Tennessee."

Down in our Essex camp,
That's where we get the cramp
Through sleeping in the damp ;
We're not allowed a lamp.
All we get there each day
Is left, right, left, right, all the way ;
Sergeants calling, lance-jacks* bawling
"Get out on parade."
We go to bed at night,
You ought to see the sight,
The earwigs on the floors
All night are forming fours.
If we're in bed in the morning,
You will hear the sergeant yawning :
"Show a leg there, show a leg there,"
'Way down in our Essex camp.

* Lance-corporals.

HOW CAN I BEAR TO LEAVE THEE? (2).
(Soldier's Farewell).

Ne'ermore may I behold thee,
Or to this heart enfold thee ;
With spear and pennon glancing,
I see the foe advancing.
    Farewell, farewell my own true love,
    Farewell, farewell my own true love.

BY KIND PERMISSION OF THE PUBLISHERS. MESSRS. J. CURWEN & SONS. 24. BERNERS STREET, W.
BAMFORTH (COPYRIGHT).

# IT'S A LONG, LONG WAY TO TIPPERARY

Written and Composed by

JACK JUDGE & HARRY WILLIAMS

Sing-ing songs of Pic-ca-dil-ly, Strand and Leicester Square, Till
"If I make mis-takes in 'spell-ing', Mol-ly dear," said he, "Re-
Leave the Strand and Pic-ca-dil-ly, or you'll be to blame, For

Pad-dy got ex-cit-ed, then he shout-ed to them there:—
-mem-ber it's the pen that's bad, don't lay the blame on me."
love has fair-ly drove me sil-ly— hop-ing you're the same!"

CHORUS

"It's a long way___ to Tip-per-ar — y,___ It's a long way___

p—f

___ to go;___ It's a long way___ to Tip-per-ar — y,___

55

To the sweet-est girl I know! Good bye Pic-ca-dil-ly, Fare-well Leicester Square, It's a long, long way to Tip-per-ar-y But my heart's right there!" It's a there!"

### Tipperary Days

Oh, weren't they the fine boys! You never saw the beat of them,
Singing altogether with their throats bronze-bare;
Fighting-fit and mirth-mad, music in the feet of them,
Swinging on to glory and the wrath out there.
Laughing by and chaffing by, frolic in the smiles of them,
On the road, the white road, all the afternoon;
Strangers in a strange land, miles and miles and miles of them,
Battle-bound and heart-high, and singing this tune:

> *It's a long way to Tipperary,*
> *It's a long way to go;*
> *It's a long way to Tipperary,*
> *And the sweetest girl I know.*
> *Goodbye, Piccadilly,*
> *Farewell, Leicester Square:*
> *It's a long, long way to Tipperary,*
> *But my heart's right there.*

Come Yvonne and Juliette! Come Mimi and cheer for them!
Throw them flowers and kisses as they pass you by.
Aren't they the lovely lads! Haven't you a tear for them,
Going out so gallantly to dare and die?
What is it they're singing so? Some high hymn of Mothérland?
Some immortal chanson of their Faith and King?
Marseillaise or Brabançon, anthem of that other land,
Dears, let us remember it, that song they sing:

> *C'est un chemin long 'to Tepararee',*
> *C'est un chemin long, c'est vrai;*
> *C'est un chemin long 'to Tepararee',*
> *Et la belle fille qu'je connais;*
>
> *Bonjour, Peekadeely!*
> *Au revoir, Lestaire Squaire!*
> *C'est un chemin long 'to Tepararee',*
> *Mais mon coeur 'ees zaire'.*

The gallant old 'Contemptibles'! There isn't much remains of them,
So full of fun and fitness, and a-singing in their pride;
For some are cold as clabber and the corby picks the brains of them,
And some are back in Blighty, and a-wishing they had died.
Ah me! It seems but yesterday, that great, glad sight of them,
Swinging on to battle as the sky grew black and black;
Yet oh, their glee and glory, and the great, grim fight of them! –
Just whistle Tipperary and it all comes back:

> *It's a long way to Tipperary*
> *(Which means 'ome anywhere);*
> *It's a long way to Tipperary*
> *(And the things wot make you care).*
> *Goodbye, Piccadilly,*
> *('Ow I 'opes my folks is well);*
> *It's a long, long way to Tipperary –*
> *('R! Aint war just 'ell?)*

ROBERT SERVICE

> *It took a long time to get it hairy,*
> *'Twas a long time to grow ;*
> *Took a long time to get it hairy,*
> *For the toothbrush hairs to show.*
> *Good-bye, Charlie Chaplin,*
> *Farewell, tufts of hair ;*
> *'Twas a long, long time to get it hairy,*
> *But now my lip's quite bare.*

HIS MASTER'S VOICE

# THE KING SIGNS ARMY

**All Irishmen to Stand Shoulder to Shoulder.**

## SIR E. GREY'S GRAVE STATEMENT.

"Could Not Stand Aside If French Channel Coast Was Bombarded."

**BANK HOLIDAY EXTENDED TO THREE DAYS.**

"Navy and Army Never at a Higher Mark."

**BELGIAN KING'S WIRE.**

## DUBLIN REVOLT

### "ON THE VERGE OF COLLAPSE."

OFFICIAL STATE-MENT.

REBEL LEADER SAID TO BE KILLED.

POST OFFICE BURNED DOWN.

REPORTED OFFERS OF SURRENDER.

BAYONET CHARGES

DOOM OF THE "IRISH REPUBLIC."

**IT'S A LONG, LONG WAY TO TIPPERARY (1).**

Up to mighty London came an Irishman one day,
As the streets are paved with gold, sure ev'ry one was gay;
Singing songs of Piccadilly, Strand and Leicester Square,
Till Paddy got excited, then he shouted to them there:—

BAMFORTH (COPYRIGHT).    THIS SONG ON SALE EVERYWHERE IN B. FELDMAN'S 6D. EDITIONS.

That's the wrong way to tickle Marie,
That's the wrong way to kiss:
Don't you know that over here, lad,
They like it better like this.
Hooray *pour la France!*
Farewell, *Angleterre!*
We didn't know the way to tickle Marie,
But now we've learnt how.

**IT'S A LONG, LONG WAY TO TIPPERARY (2).**

"It's a long way to Tipperary, it's a long way to go;
It's a long way to Tipperary, to the sweetest girl I know;
Good-bye Piccadilly, farewell Leicester Square,
It's a long, long way to Tipperary, but my heart's right there."

THERE once was a gay cavalero,
An exceedingly gay cavalero,
Who had a great friend called Miralto Me Ree
Miralto, Miralto, Miralto Me Ree.

He went to a low-down cafero,
An exceedingly low-down cafero,
And of course he took with him Miralto Me Ree
Miralto, Miralto, Miralto Me Ree.

He met there a gay signorita,
An exceedingly gay signorita,
She took a fancy to Miralto Me Ree,
Miralto, Miralto, Miralto Me Ree.

Beware, all ye gay cavalero,
Oh, beware, all ye gay cavalero,
Who value at all friend Miralto Me Ree,
Miralto, Miralto, Miralto Me Ree.

Taffy's got his Gwynnie in Glamorgan,

Jock has got his Mary in Dundee;

While Michael O'Leary

Thinks of his Dearie

Far across the Irish Sea.

Billy's got his Lilly up in London,

So the boys march on with smiles;

For every Tommy's got a girl somewhere,

In the dear old British Isles.

# MOBILISATION ORDER.

## IT'S A LONG, LONG WAY TO TIPPERARY (3).

Paddy wrote a letter to his Irish Molly O',
Saying, "Should you not receive it, write and let me
know !
If I make mistakes in spelling, Molly, dear," said he,
"Remember it's the pen that's bad, don't lay the
blame on me."

BAMFORTH (COPYRIGHT).      THIS SONG ON SALE EVERYWHERE IN B. FELDMAN'S 6d. EDITIONS.

## IT'S A LONG, LONG WAY TO TIPPERARY (4).

Molly wrote a neat reply to Irish Paddy O',
Saying, "Mike Maloney wants to marry me, and so
Leave the Strand and Piccadilly, or you'll be to blame,
For love has fairly drove me silly, hoping you're the
same."

BAMFORTH (COPYRIGHT).      THIS SONG ON SALE EVERYWHERE IN B. FELDMAN'S 6d. EDITIONS.

## Matey

### By Patrick MacGill.

*Not comin' back to-night, matey,*
  *And reliefs are comin' through,*
*We're all goin' out all right, matey,*
  *Only we're leavin' you.*
*Gawd ! it's a bloody sin, matey,*
  *Now that we've finished the fight,*
*We go when reliefs come in, matey,*
  *But you're stayin' 'ere to-night.*

*Over the top is cold, matey—*
  *You lie on the field alone,*
*Didn't I love you of old, matey,*
  *Dearer than blood of my own.*
*You were my dearest chum, matey—*
  *(Gawd ! but your face is white)*
*But now, though reliefs 'ave come, matey,*
  *I'm goin' alone to-night.*

*I'd sooner the bullet was mine, matey—*
  *Goin' out on my own,*
*Leavin' you 'ere in the line, matey,*
  *All by yourself, alone.*
*Chum o' mine and you're dead, matey,*
  *And this is the way we part.*
*The bullet went through your head, matey,*
  *But, Gawd ! it went through my 'eart.*

## "IT'S A LONG, LONG WAY TO——"

An officer's sketch of a mine leading out of the fire-trench, showing a miner going down to
the face. The mine goes about thirty yards into the field in front of our trench.

# A WINTER'S NIGHT ON THE SOMME

ANOTHER hundred yards, then a halt. " Send back to find out if the men are all in, sergeant - major." The message filters slowly back and forward; it is ten minutes before a gruff " All in " puts us on the move again. Swish, swish, swish! Will we ever strike a dry patch ? Past gleaming artillery dug-outs—

nothing doing for the gunners to-night—over mounds of earth blown in by shell-fire, we gradually work our way up to the trenches proper. Through a litter of disused cooking places and we hit George Street. Now our troubles really commence. George Street isn't boarded—it is merely mud. Down we go into it, both feet. Half France persists in clinging to our boots. Squelch, squelch, squelch ! Surely there is no mud on earth to equal trench mud.

WIRES, wires everywhere. Those artillery-men of ours seem to think trenches were made only to strew thousands of wires through. Criss-cross, underfoot, overhead, they trip our feet, catch us stingingly under the nose, lift our " tin hats " off; God knows what they don't do. In our imagination we invest them

with the powers of a thousand devils. Slower and slower the pace becomes ; a continual stream of profanity penetrates the sodden atmosphere. " Oxford Circus," off to the right here. We are in the second line now ; will-o'-the-wisp lights shine out of the ground, and we pass recumbent forms on firesteps, occasional sentries who take not the slightest notice of us. What does it matter ? I take a look over the parapet. A damp mist rising slowly upward from the valley on our right ; a profound, brooding stillness.

Only the indefatigable machine-gunner is at work ; the crash of his gun echoes through the surrounding ridges like the beat of the surf on a Pacific beach. Off to the left here. I give the men a breather—they want it badly—and take the opportunity to go into battalion headquarters, report my presence, and have a welcome whisky-and-soda.

ON again ; we meet a working-party of pioneers coming out. Their picks and shovels batter away the few remaining remnants of our patience ; they squeeze past to a chorus of cheerful prognostications as to their ultimate destination in life. Forward again, a short halt to find a trench to make tea in—Lord only knows how it is to be done—through a narrow sap and we have reached the part of the line we are to take over.

O.C. COMPANY to be relieved is no sluggard ; his haste, in fact, is rather indecent. His men are all waiting on the firesteps, packs on, to facilitate our progress. Bombs here, ammunition there, Boche over yonder, and before we know where we are the relieved have collected their belongings, bestowed fervent blessings and wishes of good luck on us and filed slowly out of the trench. Well, good luck to them ; they've done their share. Now to get the men settled down. " Sergeant-major." " Yessir," answers that faithful functionary. " What about getting the sentries posted ? " " All done, sir." (The Q.-M. is one of the Kaiser's " contemptibles.") " Right ; let us go along and have a look at them."

So collecting the platoon officers, we pass through our bit of the line. We have to " live " here for a week—perhaps more. Much remains to be done before we are anything like comfortable. Plenty of charcoal for the braziers, too. We are in luck's way to-night. The audible grousings and mutterings die slowly away ; we find each man somewhere to deposit himself and his belongings. The men crowd round, mess-tin in hand, indulge in the usual grouse should one have a trifle less than the other, and then drift slowly back to the red glow of the braziers. In and around the nooks and crannies, a long last look over the top and we bid the sergeant - major good-night and crawl down to our dug-out.

A winter's night on the Somme. Think of it, you people of England ; think of it as you lie in your warm, comfortable beds. Think of the men " holding the line," holding it amidst hail, rain and snow, and thank God you possess such men. "O. Pip."

## from DEATH'S MEN

The men of death stand trim and neat,
   Their faces stiff as stone,
Click, clack, go four and twenty feet
   From twelve machines of bone.


'Click, clack, left, right, form fours, incline',
   The jack-box sergeant cries;
For twelve erect and wooden dolls
   One clockwork doll replies.


And twelve souls wander 'mid still clouds
   In a land of snow-drooped trees,
Faint, foaming streams fall in grey hills
   Like beards on old men's knees.

Old men, old hills, old kings their beards
   Cold stone-grey still cascades
Hung high above this shuddering earth
   Where the red blood sinks and fades.


Then the quietness of all ancient things,
   Their round and full repose
As balm upon twelve wandering souls
   Down from the grey sky flows.


The rooks from out the tall gaunt trees
   In shrieking circles pass;
Click, clack, click, clack, go Death's trim men
   Across the Autumn grass.

W. J. TURNER

### TIP-TOP TIPPERARY MARY (1).

Tipperary Tommy was a soldier boy, brave as any lad could be;
Tipperary Mary was a pretty lass, waiting for her Tommy
        'cross the sea;
In her heart, in her heart a beating feeling tells of a
        love that is all true blue,
And in her ear a song Tommy sang will linger long, and
        thrill her thro' and thro.'

### TIP-TOP TIPPERARY MARY (2).

Tip-top Tipperary Mary, I love you true,
Tip-top Tipperary Mary, my love's true as your eyes of blue;
I dream of your endearing young charms ev'ry night thro',
Tho' I'm far away from Tipperary, Mary, my heart's with you.

### TIP-TOP TIPPERARY MARY (3).

Tipperary Tommy, so the story goes, told a comrade one
        dark night,
" Ev'rything is fading, it's myself that knows, never ever-
        more will Tommy fight;
In my heart, in my heart a throbbing seems to tell of
        my Mary so far away,
When you go marching home, sing to Mary 'cross the foam,
        this song I sang one day."

## The Lady Fair

Tune : "Brighton Camp" or "The girl I left behind me."

THERE's a lady fair in a barrack square,
And it's rather a job to find her,
'Cos there's Grenadier Guards all round her neck,
And the Fusiliers behind her.

62

arkness: the rain sluiced down; the mire was deep;
 was past twelve on a mid-winter night,
hen peaceful folk in beds lay snug asleep;
here, with much work to do before the light,
Ve lugged our clay-sucked boots as best we might
 long the trench; sometimes a bullet sang,
nd droning shells burst with a hollow bang;
Ve were soaked, chilled and wretched, every one;
arkness; the distant wink of a huge gun.

urned in the black ditch, loathing the storm;
 rocket fizzed and burned with blanching flare,
nd lit the face of what had been a form
oundering in mirk. He stood before me there;
ay that He was Christ; stiff in the glare,
nd leaning forward from His burdening task,
oth arms supporting it; His eyes on mine
ared from the woeful head that seemed a mask
f mortal pain in Hell's unholy shine.

o thorny crown, only a woollen cap
e wore—an English soldier, white and strong,
Vho loved his time like any simple chap,
ood days of work and sport and homely song;
ow he has learned that nights are very long,
nd dawn a watching of the windowed sky.
ut to the end, unjudging, he'll endure
lorror and pain, not uncontent to die
hat Lancaster on Lune may stand secure.

le faced me, reeling in his weariness,
houldering his load of planks, so hard to bear.
say that He was Christ, who wrought to bless
ll groping things with freedom bright as air,
nd with His mercy washed and made them fair.
hen the flame sank, and all grew black as pitch,
Vhile we began to struggle along the ditch;
nd someone flung his burden in the muck,
Iumbling: 'O Christ Almighty, now I'm struck!'

*Siegfried Sassoon*

### PLUCKY BRITISHER.

Here is a story of a pathetic incident which took place little longer ago. It was in February, when the people of Ghent saw a solitary British soldier, well set-up and athletic looking, being marched through the streets in charge of three German soldiers with fixed bayonets.

The British soldier was hatless, but he was smoking a cigarette with evident enjoyment. One woman ran out and wanted to give the soldier a cap, but the guards moved her away. That could not be allowed without orders from headquarters.

All were sympathetic to the soldier, till at last one poor woman burst out crying at the sight of the prisoner. The soldier saw, took his cigarette from his mouth, and with a smile he called out:—

"Don't cry, mother, I've killed twenty-five of them."

"What did you say?" asked the German guard.

And the soldier replied in broken French 'I was asking the way to Tipperary."

"Farther on, at the Kommandetour office No. 6," answered the guard, satisfied.

### GOOD THINGS IN A GERMAN TRENCH.

Private Walter Birchall, of the 5th King's (Liverpool Regiment), writing home, says:—

"You will have read in the papers of the battle last Sunday. Our boys were properly in. They were over the top this time and did themselves credit. I pray to God I shall never see anything like it again. It was hell while it was on. When the position was taken and the Germans found it all up with them, they ran towards us with white flags, saying, "You English is good. We don't wan to fight against you." We took a lot of prisoners, and when we took their trenches our boys had a good time. You talk about them starving! Why, we found cigars, champagne, bread, German sausage, chocolate, and everything."

Last night as I lay on my pillow,
Last night as I lay on my bed,
I dreamt our old corp'ral was dying,
I dreamt the old buffer was dead.

*Chorus*

Send him,
Oh, send him,
Oh, send our old corp'ral to He-e-ll;
Oh, keep him,
Oh, keep him,
Oh, keep the old buffer in Hell.

## OXO at the Front
### CONTENTED CANADIANS
A Sergeant in Princess Patricia's Canadian Regiment writes:—

At last we are where we wanted to be and are contented with our little lot. We had a fairly good Christmas. Dinner consisted of bully beef and biscuits and whatever we could forage. My friend, Sergeant ——, and myself did not do so badly, as we had 1 carrot, ½ turnip, 2 leeks, 1 onion, **OXO,** and 12 oz. of bully beef, with three hard biscuits, all mixed up and boiled in a bully beef tin. It sure made a tasty dinner. We are all in good spirits, and also within sound of the big guns.

*Reprinted from "The Daily Mail,"*
*Jan. 7th, 1915.*

### Scottish soldier's cheery letter.

"In one billet our mess kitchen was partly blown away with a shell, and the old thatch made a comfortable shakedown. Seven of us mixed up dinners and messed out of one tin— potatoes from the pit, bully beef, **OXO** and hard biscuits—which we enjoyed immensely."

*From the Glasgow "Daily Record,"*
*Jan. 4th, 1915.*

*Reprinted from "Carlisle Journal,"*
*Nov. 13th, 1914.*

"Yesterday morning I had 31 patients —slightly sick, sprained ankles, and such like. I discharged 12 of them to duty in the afternoon. At 6.30 I had to stand ready to get in cases brought down in motor ambulances from a hospital nearer the front. I saw them all in, had hot **OXO** and bread for them, and went up for my dinner, got back about nine o'clock, and then started to dress the cases needing it most."

## MECHANISED TRANSPORT

One morning someone came round and was asking for volunteers to join the cyclist mob. I gave one look at my pile of goods on the floor and said 'Tom, my old cock, you're in'. The next day I fell in with the trick cyclists and pushed off on foot, plus all our supermarket stuff on our back. I'd have given fifty francs for a wheel barrow, if I'd had the money. At last, nearly sold out, we came to an Ordnance Store, the excitement was great as they wheeled out the 'iron horses', B.S.A.'s, brand spanking new. I signed for mine with an air of a big pot signing a peace treaty. It was posh, clips for the rifle and a carrier for the kit complete with puncture outfit and a new pump, I like the others, started to pack our worldly goods on the carrier, yes there were also two straps fixed on the carrier. I only being a short bloke, by the time I had got my stuff packed on the back found I had a job to cock my leg over to mount — what with the weight of the bike and old French cobbled roads we started our wobbly ride to an unknown destination. I thought to myself if Jerry was to capture us now, he would let us go. At last after feeling quite stiff and wondering if I had done the right thing, the officer in front blew his whistle and put up his hand. This I took for the signal to fall

off, which I did, and flopped down by the side of the road, while the officers laid out their maps, talking to each other, pointing to the way we had come and the way we were going and shaking their heads. I began to wonder if we were even in the right country where the war was supposed to be.

After about 10 minutes the Captain in charge made a smiling tour along the line of his noble troops asking if we were all right etc., and telling us we would make camp within the hour. I gave one more look at my bike and wondered if we ever would be pals. After what seemed a lifetime we came to a farm, same whist and raised arm, and again I fell off with the others. We were instructed to wheel our bikes into the farmyard and stack them four deep against the wall and take off packs and rifles, make ourselves comfortable in the barn and a meal would be ready in half an hour. We found we had a field kitchen and couple of cooks at the back of the farm house and when someone shouted "come and get it" we dived out of the barn with our canteens, which were duly loaded with stew, very nice too — we were ready for it.

*from Tom Green's Journal*

IT'S A GRAND SIGHT TO SEE THEM
GOING AWAY (2).

It's a grand sight to see them going away,
A grand sight to see them going away;
Left, right, left, right, they march along,
Gaily whistling a lively song.
They don't care what they have to face,
They don't care where they have to roam;
It's a grand sight to see them going away,
But a grander sight to see them coming home.

BY ARRANGEMENT WITH MESSRS. FRANCIS, DAY & HUNTER, THE PUBLISHERS OF THE MUSIC.
BAMFORTH COPYRIGHT.

## Y.M.C.A. Treacle Roll

Tune : "The House that Jack Built."

THIS is the Roll
They sell in the Hut,
That feeds the men
That make the planes,
That swing the prop
That pulls the bus,
Right over to France.
To carry the bombers
Just over the line,
And help the Gunners
To drop the shells
Right on to the dug-out
That Fritz built.

he baths at Nieppe were in a brewery adjoining the
ver Lys.. We removed tunic and trousers and tied
em with our identity-disc cords to be put through
delousing machine. We then proceeded to the wash-
ouse across the road in full view of a foregathering
village maidens.

side, we were split into dozens, each group being
lotted to a vat, where we remained immersed up to
e neck for five glorious minutes. At 5 mins 15 sec
cold hose was turned on to roust out the laggards.
clean shirt, pants, and socks were handed out, and
these we returned to the first building.

anyone was then unable to find his deloused
ousers, he wandered around like a lost sheep until
ven a pair yards too big, which he had to wear
til he could arrange to rip them beyond repair on
e next wiring-party.

*N. Edwards*

## NO FRIVOLITY!

The anti-freeze in the handbooks was generally non-existent, so in 1915 we were directed to add rum to the contents of the water-jacket of the Maxim.

No true soldier would dream of such desecration, so we hit on a better plan. By giving the double-button a quick poke every ten minutes during a frosty night a single round could be fired which would be taken for a rifle-shot. Dexterity was essential, for two or more shots would give away the position as an MG post.

Developing from this, some adroit gunner discovered that by celerity of manipulation a gun in a known position could be fired to the tempo of Om-tiddy-pom-pom. The Germans picked it up, and would answer with a Pom-Pom.

At Ypres in 1917 I had a Vickers gunner, a violinist in civilian life, who could tap out the beat of "The Policeman's Holiday" without a fault!

Some killjoy must have made out a report of all this. An edict was issued by GHQ that "frivolous" machine-gunnery must cease forthwith. The Germans must have wondered why THEIR Om-tiddy no longer elicited the levity of an answering Pom-Pom.

*F. Jackson*

## SHIRT-SHOCKED

During the years of the static trench and gun pit warfare, some of us acquired quite a lot of spare kit from dead and wounded comrades e.g. blankets, groundsheets, socks, shirts, etc.

The sergeant-major did not approve of this spare stuff being piled on the guns and ammunition wagons, making them as he put it 'look like ruddy Christmas Trees' when the battery moved from one front to another.

It became a habit when moving to pack as much as possible down the 'piece' (the barrel of the gun) before putting on the muzzle cover. On one occasio after being on the march for a couple of days, the battery came into action on a new part of the front My kit down the barrel was forgotten.

The first round fired blew all my carefully packed socks, shirts and shaving kit to shreds out in front of the gun pit, much to the amusement of the lads and the enemy!

*C. W. Archer.*

### Prelude: the Troops

Dim, gradual thinning of the shapeless gloom
Shudders to drizzling daybreak that reveals
Disconsolate men who stamp their sodden boots
And turn dulled, sunken faces to the sky
Haggard and hopeless. They, who have beaten down
The stale despair of night, must now renew
Their desolation in the truce of dawn,
Murdering the livid hours that grope for peace.

Yet these, who cling to life with stubborn hands,
Can grin through storms of death and find a gap
In the clawed, cruel tangles of his defence.
They march from safety, and the bird-sung joy
Of grass-green thickets, to the land where all
Is ruin, and nothing blossoms but the sky
That hastens over them where they endure
Sad, smoking, flat horizons, reeking woods,
And foundered trench-lines volleying doom for doom.

O my brave brown companions, when your souls
Flock silently away, and the eyeless dead
Shame the wild beast of battle on the ridge,
Death will stand grieving in that field of war
Since your unvanquished hardihood is spent.

And through some mooned Valhalla there will pass
Battalions and battalions, scarred from hell;
The unreturning army that was youth;
The legions who have suffered and are dust.

SIEGFRIED SASSOON

## MY LITTLE WET HOLE IN THE TRENCH

...e a little wet hole in the trench
...here the rain storms continually drench;
...here's a dead cow nearby,
...ith its heels to the sky,
...nd it gives forth a horrible stench!
...nderneath us in place of a floor
...here's a mush of wet mush and straw;
...hile the Jack Johnsons they tear
...hrough the rain-sodden air,
...o my little wet hole in the trench

...ow its bully and biscuits we chew
...nd its weeks since we had a good stew;
...hile in lieu of cooked ham,
...e get Tom Ticklers jam,
... fact that is wellknown to be true.
...ow the snipers they keep on the go
...o it behoves you to keep your head low,
...hile the Jack Johnsons they tear,
...hrough the rain-sodden air,
...o your little wet hole in the trench

...n paydays when we get our pay
...o the estaminet we all make our way
...ut the beer that they sell
...akes us all run like hell
...o we make do with cafe au lait;
...nd the French Girl who serves us says 'Oui'!
...hile she's bubbling all over with glee;
...nd as sure as you're born
...ou'll return so forlorn,
...o your little wet hole in the trench.

*...euben Bray*

...ow we've been out in Flanders for many a weary day,
...marching and a-fighting in the good old British way,
...e don't complain of nothing, but we'd dearly like to
      know
...fore we are Napootaloo, what for? where to? we go?

## The Infantryman.

THE gunner rides on horseback, he lives in luxury,
  The sapper has his dug-out as cushy as can be,
The flying man's a sportsman, but his home's a long way back,
In painted tent or straw-spread barn or cosy little shack,
Gunner and sapper and flying man (and each to his job, say I)
Have tickled the Hun with mine or gun or bombed him from on
      high,
But the quiet work, and the dirty work, since ever the war began
Is the work that never shows at all, the work of the infantryman.

The guns can pound the villages and smash the trenches in,
And the Hun is fain for home again when the T.M.B.'s begin,
And the Vickers gun is a useful one to sweep a parapet.
But the real work is the work that's done with bomb and bayonet.
Load him down from heel to crown with tools and grub and kit,
He's always there where the fighting is—he's there unless he's
      hit ;
Over the mud and the blasted earth he goes where the living can ;
He's in at the death while he yet has breath, the British infantry-
      man !

Trudge and slip on the Shell-hole's lip, and fall in the clinging
      mire—
Steady in front, go steady ! Close up there ! Mind the wire !
Double behind where the pathways wind ! Jump clear of the
      ditch, jump clear !
Lost touch at the back ? Oh, halt in front, and duck when the
      shells come near !

Carrying parties all night long, all day in a muddy trench,
With your feet in the wet and your head in the rain, and the
      sodden khaki's stench !
Then over the top in the morning, and onward all you can—
This is the work that wins the war, the work of the infantryman.

"Punch," 31st January, 1917.

## THE OLD ROUTINE

I had just filled a sandbag and placed it on the top of the parapet when I happened to glance down, and saw a slight movement in the earth between my feet. I stooped and scraped away the soil with my fingers and found what seemed like palpitating flesh. It proved to be a man's cheek, and a few minutes' work uncovered his head. I poured a little water down his throat, and two or three of us dug out the rest of him. He was undamaged except for his feet and ankles, which were a mass of pulp, and he recovered consciousness as we worked. The first thing he said was in English: 'What Corps are you?' He was a big man, and told us he was forty-five and had only been a soldier for a fortnight.

We dragged him out and laid him under the hedge. There was nothing else we could do for him. He had another drink later, but he must have died in the course of the day. I am afraid we forgot all about him, but nothing could have lived there until evening.

The Captain was the next to go. He insisted on standing on the parados, directing operations, and got a bullet in the lungs. He could walk, and two men were detailed to take him down to the dressing-station. One came back, to be killed later in the day, but the other stopped a bullet *en route* and followed the Captain.

When we had got our big Hun out, he left a big hole in the ground, and we found a dead arm and hand projecting from the bottom. We dug about, but did not seem to be able to find the body, and when I seized the sleeve and pulled, the arm came out of the ground by itself. We had to dig deeper for our own sake, but there was nothing else left, except messy earth, which seemed to have been driven into the side of the trench. The man helping me turned sick, for it wasn't pretty work, but I claimed a substitute, and between us we carted out a barrowful in wetter sheets and dumped it under the hedge. After that I had had enough myself.

*H. S. Clapham*

## Tommie's Philosophy at the Front.

"WHEN you are a soldier, you are one of two things, either you are at the front or you are behind the lines, you need not worry. If you are at the front you are one of two things. You are either in a danger zone or you are not. If you are not, you need not worry. If you are in a danger zone you are one of two things. You are either wounded or you are not. If you are wounded you need not worry. If you are wounded you are one of two things. You are either seriously wounded or slightly wounded. If you are slightly wounded you need not worry. If you are seriously wounded one of two things is certain. Either you get well or you die. If you get well you need not worry. If you die you can't worry. Therefore, there is no need to worry at all."

**J. J. L. SAINT ONGE.**

# Is it Coming to This.

THE Kaiser has been at it again. This time he predicts that force of arms will bring the war to a close by August. But [h]e does not state whose arms or in which year. Let us be [m]agnanimous, however, and assume (O huge assumption !) that [h]e is in earnest and means this year. The mighty of the Central [p]owers are preparing to be '' put down from their seats.'' What [sh]all they do for a living when the loot of war is no longer avail[ab]le ? We have an idea. They will advertise in the daily press. [A]nd we expect to see something like the following :

The SULTAN MEHMED respectfully informs his friends [(a]nd others) that pressing necessity has compelled him to remove [to] more commodious premises on the other side of the Bosphorus, [w]here he will carry on his high-class Butchering Business as [u]sual. Armenian Papers please copy.

GENERAL VON BISSING, sometime Governor of Belgium, [h]as opened a kindergarten. Special attention given to refractory [c]hildren. Modern methods of Kultur. Splendid results in [B]russels, Antwerp, etc.

If the G.O. COMMANDING MESS O' POTAMIAN ARMIES [w]ill call at the Imperial Palace, Potsdam, he will hear little to his [a]dvantage.

Why do your own dirty work ? Let us do it for you. Wide [e]xperience. FOXEY, FERDINAND and Co., SOFIA.

Authors ! Authors ! ! Authors ! ! ! Inventors of tall [s]tories invited to communicate with the WOLFF PRESS GANG, [B]ERLIN.

WILLIAM HOHENZOLLERN has a Past that he is anxious [t]o part with. No offer refused.

LITTLE, WILLIE and Co., Expert House-Breakers. Libraries, [M]useums, Art Galleries, Residences, dismantled at short notice. [C]ontractors by Self-appointment to the University of Louvain.

COUNT ZEPPELIN, having gone down to a warmer climate, [c]an no more go up to a colder. Number of new and huge stock [o]f damaged machines for sale. Perfect safety guaranteed [e]xcept in envirous of Paris, Salonica, and the East Coast of [E]ngland.

Open for engagements. The world-famed wizard, MAXI[MI]LIAN HARDEN. Positively the only man who has ever [su]cceeded in making $2 \times 2 = 5$.

A. G. BARKER.
J. Q. ADAMS.

## Optimist and Pessimist

OPTIMIST. I love the land of " La Belle France."
PESSIMIST. What ! Ypres and the Somme ?
O.     I love to travel all around,
P.     And I want to go home,
O.     But when the great big push begins,
P.     And Drakes are going west,
O.     Why you might win a Victoria Cross,
P.     Across the channel's best.

O. & P. The Optimist and the Pessimist,
    That's what they call us two.
O.     The rations are quite good of late,
P.     It's stew, and stew, then stew.
O.     And leave is four days extra now.
P.     Aye, just when I've had mine.
O.     But still you've fourteen days to come.
P.     About nineteen-twenty-nine (1929).

O.     Cheer up, old boy, you're not dead yet,
P.     Not yet, but still there's hope,
O.     A soldier's life is not too bad,
P.     Not when you know the ropes.
O.     Remember when the fight is won,
P.     I don't think we've much chance,
O.     You'll be a hero with everyone,
P.     Or own six feet of France.

O. & P. The Optimist and the Pessimist,
    That's what they call us two.
O.     I think the war will soon be o'er,
P.     In another year or two.
O.     Then I'll get back to Blighty,
    And quaff the flowing cup,
P.     And I'll be left behind in France
    To fill the trenches up.

## GUILLEMONT.

TUNE : " Moonlight Bay."

We were rushing along
    In Guilleymong ;
We could hear the Boche a singing :
    They seemed to say,
" You have stolen our trench,
    But don't go away,
And we'll pepper you with tear shells
    All the day."

We were waiting for them
    Later on in the day ;
You might have heard our voices singing :
    " Don't lose your way.
This is your old trench,
    Now, do step this way,
And we'll give you souvenirs
    To take away."

8308

# THERE'S A LONG LONG TRAIL

The property of
ONDON STATION
BRITISH BROADCASTING CORP!

WRITTEN BY
STODDARD KING

COMPOSED BY
ZO ELLIOTT

London:
West's Ltd.
12, Moor St    Charing Cross Rd W.1.
(close to Palace Theatre)

COPYRIGHT MCMXIV
BY WEST & CO

MELBOURNE:
CHAPPELL & Cº

PRICE 2/-
NET CASH

NEW YORK:
M. WITMARK & SON.

71

# THERE'S A LONG, LONG TRAIL

Written by
STODDARD KING

Composed by
ZO. ELLIOTT

1. Nights are grow-ing ve - ry lone - ly,
2. All night long I hear you call - ing,

Days are ve - ry long;
Call - ing sweet and low;

I'm a - grow-ing wea - ry on - ly
Seem to hear your foot-steps fall - ing

list-'ning for your song. Old re - mem-brances are throng - ing
ev -'ry-where I go. Tho' the road between us stretch - es

Thro' my mem - o - ry. Throng-ing till it seems the
Man - y a wea - ry mile, Some-how I for - get that

world is full of dreams Just to call you back to me.
you're not with me yet When I think I see you smile.

**CHORUS**

Key Ab

There's a long, long trail a - wind-ing In-to the land of my dreams, Where the

night - in-gales are sing - ing And a white moon

beams: There's a long, long night of wait - ing Un-til my

dreams all come true; Till the day when I'll be

go - ing down That long, long trail with you. There's a you.

**THERE'S A LONG, LONG TRAIL (1)**

Nights are growing very lonely, Days are very long;
I'm a-growing weary only listening for your song;
Old remembrances are thronging Thro' my memory.
Thronging till it seems the world is full of dreams
Just to call you back to me.

CHORUS.

There's a long, long trail a-wind-ing In-to the land of my dreams,

By permission of Messrs West & Co., Rathbone Place, London, W.

**THERE'S A LONG, LONG TRAIL (2)**

All night long I hear you calling, Calling sweet and low;
Seem to hear your footsteps falling everywhere I go.
Tho' the road between us stretches Many a weary mile,
Somehow I forget that you're not with me yet
When I think I see you smile.

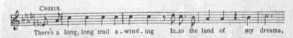

CHORUS.

There's a long, long trail a-wind-ing In-to the land of my dreams,

By permission of Messrs West & Co., Rathbone Place, London, W.

## Rendezvous

I have a rendezvous with Death
At some disputed barricade,
When Spring comes back with rustling shade
And apple-blossoms fill the air –
I have a rendezvous with Death
When Spring brings back blue days and fair.

It may be he shall take my hand
And lead me into his dark land
And close my eyes and quench my breath –
It may be I shall pass him still.
I have a rendezvous with Death
On some scarred slope of battered hill,
When Spring comes round again this year
And the first meadow-flowers appear.

God knows 'twere better to be deep
Pillowed in silk and scented down,
Where love throbs out in blissful sleep,
Pulse nigh to pulse, and breath to breath,
Where hushed awakenings are dear . . .
But I've a rendezvous with Death
At midnight in some flaming town,
When Spring trips north again this year,
And I to my pledged word am true,
I shall not fail that rendezvous.

ALAN SEEGER
*killed in action, 1916*

**THERE'S A LONG, LONG TRAIL** *(Refrain)*

There's a long, long trail a-winding Into the land of my dreams,
Where the nightingales are singing And a white moon beams;
There a long, long night of waiting, Until my dreams all come true,
Till the day when I'll be going down That long, long trail with you.

CHORUS.

There's a long, long trail a-wind-ing In-to the land of my dreams,

By permission of Messrs West & Co., Rathbone Place, London, W.

# A Long, Long Trail

THERE are soldiers in the trenches,
Thinking of their home,
Waiting patiently and wondering when the end will come,
Old remembrances are thronging through their memories;
But in all their dreams, covering many themes,
They think sometimes like this:

There's a long, long sound of whining
In the midst of my dreams,
O'er the long, long trenches winding, from the
coast on past Rheims,
There's a long, long time of waiting, until my dreams
all come true,
Till the day that I am marching back, that sweet
homeland to view.

Now Jack, he leads upon the sea a different sort of life,
But there are also times when he thinks not only of strife,
But wonders when will be the time the trail will lead to
home,
But he'll not forget, though he's not there yet, and
sometimes he will hum:

There's a long, long trail of sailing, on seas all the
world o'er,
There's a deep, deep cry of wailing for those who
are no more,
There's a long, long time of waiting until my
dreams all come true,
Till the day that I am sailing back, that sweet
homeland to view.

Those flying about up in the air, 'midst danger every
minute,
'Midst birds that sing so sweetly there, the lark and the
linnet,
Oft-times will they wish themselves back again at home,
Yet on the wing they'll cheerily sing, until that time
may come:

There's a long, long trail of flying, though shells
may crash and whine,
There'll be a long, long day of joying when we get
o'er the Rhine,
There's a long, long time of waiting until my
dreams all come true,
Till the day that I am flying back, that sweet homeland to view.

THE LONG, LONG TRAIL: COMING BACK FROM A ROUTE MARCH

## FLOTSAM

I can still see a couple of young girls, sisters perhaps,
helping each other, hardly able to drag themselves
along, the blood from their torn feet oozing through
their low silk shoes: a very sick woman, who
looked as if she were dying, balanced somehow on a
perambulator; a paralytic old man in a wheelbarrow,
pushed by his sturdy daughter; a very old, very
respectable couple, who for years had probably
done no more than walk arm-in-arm round a small
garden, now, still arm-in-arm, were helping each
other in utter bewilderment of mind and exhaus-
tion of body down the long meaningless road. I
remember, too, a small boy playing the man and
encouraging his mother, and an exhausted woman
sinking under the weight of her two babies.
And none might stop: the gendarmes pounced on
any who tarried and shoved them forward. The mass
of refugees must be kept on the move. If they
halted they would hopelessly block the communications they were already so seriously encumbering.
Later, perhaps, it would become necessary to drive
them off the roads into the fields, to clear the way
for the troops, so on they had to stagger, men and
tired cattle together, with here and there a huge
cart drawn by oxen, packed with children. Some
of these carts must have contained the entire
infant population of a village thrown in pell-mell.
Were their parents trudging behind, or had they
fallen by the way? The column of civilians must go
endlessly on, whoever might drop out or get left
behind, on and on and on, a wretched, racked,
miserable mass of humanity, whose motive
power was fear, and whose urge was a sound, the
dull rumble of guns, ominously near, growling
ceaselessly to the north.

Whenever there came a particularly sharp burst of
artillery fire rending the air like a sudden thunder-
clap, the whole miserable column trembled and
staggered forward, all but the oxen moving faster
for a moment, then relapsing into the former slow
drag.

*E. L. Spears*

## DEATH WITHOUT GLORY

*Aug.* In a meadow, close to the river, on the left
bank of the Yadir, just below the inn of Krivaia, I
saw the following spectacle:

A group of children, girls, women, and men, 15 in
all, were lying dead, tied together by their hands.
Most of them had been bayoneted. One young
girl had been bayoneted below the jaw, on the left,
and the point of the weapon had come out through
the right cheek-bone. Many of the corpses had no
teeth left. On the back of an old woman who was
lying on her face, there was some coagulated
blood, and in this were found some teeth. This
old woman was lying beside the girl whose wound
has been described above. It would appear that
the old woman was killed first, and the young girl
immediately afterwards, so that the teeth of the
latter were scattered on the back of the old woman.
The chemises of the little girls and young women
were blood-stained, which seems to indicate that
they were violated before being killed. Near this
group, apart, lay the dead bodies of three men
who had been bayoneted in the head, throat, and
cheek.

*Colonel Dokitch — Report on atrocities committed
by the Austro-Hungarian army*

## BLIND

3 a.m. of a hot, still night.

'No, Nurse, I can't sleep. Sit with me a little, Nurse.'

The words were whispered very low. Down the long length of the ward no one else was stirring, and the bed in which the speaker lay had screens all round it. He had not been long in Hospital, and he was more ill than he knew, being threatened with tetanus and quite blind; but it was only this morning they had told him of his blindness.

'When will you take away the bandages so that I can *SEE?*

Those were the words he always said at the conclusion of each dressing. 'I do want to *SEE.* Why, I haven't ever seen you, Nurse,' and he would laugh, as though the remark was of real humour. But today they broke it to him, and in the little kitchen off the ward, I listened while his day-nurse told me.

'How did he take it?' I asked at length.

She shook her head. 'Just asked if they were certain there was no hope - that was all. But he hasn't spoken since.'

So I waited beside him, a little draught blowing upon us from an open window near.

'Nurse, you know I'm to be blind - always?'
'Yes,' I answered, and took one of his hands in mine. But after a little while I drew a chair beside his bed and we talked in whispers about France, for it amused him to describe some of the strange places in which he had been billeted. Then he was hungry, and I fed him with hot buttered toast and hot milk, much sweetened. It was difficult to find his mouth in the darkness, and he always laughed, a funny little husky laugh, when crumbs went up his nose.

'It will be a month tomorrow since I was hit,' he said as he crunched the last piece of toast. 'All that time before is like a quite different life. It **is** queer.' Then he added, and again he gave that husky little laugh, 'Nurse, I say, you won't forget my early morning tea. You know you did forget it yesterday,' and with the last words he stretched his hand towards me, his way of discovering if I am offended.

He died yesterday morning, the blind boy I had become so fond of. A concert was in progress, and for a while after they had told me, I stood idle and listened to the singing.

> "There's a long, long trail a-winding,
> Into the land of my dreams,
> Where the nightingales are singing,
> And the pale moon gleams."

It echoes still in my ears, that wailing, aching chorus of the "Long, Long Trail." All the men were singing it, and there, beneath the window where I had grown so used to the sight of blue draped screens, was an empty bed - white and fresh, a suit of pyjamas beneath the pillows - waiting for another occupant.

*M. V. Woodgate*
*The English Churchwoman*

# 10 MILES OF DEAD ON FIELD. BATTLE CARPET

# NINE MILES OF TRENCHES ARE FILLED WITH DEAD AS VON KLUCK'S ARMY TURNS

## DIED OF WOUNDS

His wet white face and miserable eyes
Brought nurses to him more than groans and sighs:
But hoarse and low and rapid rose and fell
His troubled voice; he did the business well.

The ward grew dark; but he was still complaining
And calling out for 'Dickie'. 'Curse the Wood!
It's time to go. O Christ, and what's the good?
We'll never take it, and it's always raining.'

I wondered where he'd been; then heard him shout,
'They snipe like hell! O Dickie, don't go out' . . .
I fell asleep . . . Next morning he was dead;
And some Slight Wound lay smiling on the bed.

*Siegfried Sassoon*

## LAMENTATIONS

I found him in the guard-room at the Base.
From the blind darkness I had heard his crying
And blundered in. With puzzled, patient face
A sergeant watched him; it was no good trying
To stop it; for he howled and beat his chest.
And, all because his brother had gone west,
Raved at the bleeding war; his rampant grief
Moaned, shouted, sobbed, and choked, while he was kneeling
Half-naked on the floor. In my belief
Such men have lost all patriotic feeling.

*Siegfried Sassoon*

FIGHT THE GOOD FIGHT (4)
FAINT NOT, NOR FEAR, HIS ARMS
ARE NEAR:
HE CHANGETH NOT, AND THOU ART DEAR;
ONLY BELIEVE, AND THOU SHALT SEE
THAT CHRIST IS ALL IN ALL TO THEE.
BAMFORTH (Copyright).

AT ST. DUNSTAN'S, REGENT'S PARK : A CHEERFUL PARTY OF BLIND SOLDIERS

### Dulce et Decorum est

Bent double, like old beggars under sacks,
Knock-kneed, coughing like hags, we cursed through sludge,
Till on the haunting flares we turned our backs,
And towards our distant rest began to trudge.
Men marched asleep. Many had lost their boots,
But limped on, blood-shod. All went lame, all blind;
Drunk with fatigue; deaf even to the hoots
Of gas-shells dropping softly behind.

Gas! Gas! Quick, boys! – An ecstasy of fumbling,
Fitting the clumsy helmets just in time,
But someone still was yelling out and stumbling
And floundering like a man in fire or lime. –
Dim through the misty panes and thick green light,
As under a green sea, I saw him drowning.

In all my dreams, before my helpless sight,
He plunges at me, guttering, choking, drowning.

If in some smothering dreams, you too could pace
Behind the wagon that we flung him in,
And watch the white eyes writhing in his face,
His hanging face, like a devil's sick of sin;
If you could hear, at every jolt, the blood
Come gargling from the froth-corrupted lungs,
Obscene as cancer, bitter as the cud
Of vile, incurable sores on innocent tongues, –
My friend, you would not tell with such high zest
To children ardent for some desperate glory,
The old Lie: Dulce et decorum est
Pro patria mori.

WILFRED OWEN
*killed in action, 1918*

## CAUGHT BY HIS OWN GAS.

### ATTEMPTED ATTACK ON BRITISH LINES.

*Hindenburg's Line.*

## Before Action

By all the glories of the day
   And the cool evening's benison,
By that last sunset touch that lay
   Upon the hills when day was done,
By beauty lavishly outpoured
   And blessings carelessly received,
By all the days that I have lived
   Make me a soldier, Lord.

By all of man's hopes and fears,
   And all the wonders poets sing,
The laughter of unclouded years,
   And every sad and lovely thing;
By the romantic ages stored
   With high endeavour that was his,
By all his mad catastrophes
   Make me a man, O Lord.

I, that on my familiar hill
   Saw with uncomprehending eyes
A hundred of Thy sunsets spill
   Their fresh and sanguine sacrifice,

Ere the sun swings his noonday sword
   Must say goodbye to all of this; –
By all delights that I shall miss,
   Help me to die, O Lord.

              W. N. HODGSON
        *written two days before his*
          *death on July 1st, 1916*

Now the pipes are playing, now the drums are beat,
Now the strong battalions are marching up the street,
But the pipes will not be playing and the bayonets will not shine,
When the regiments I dream of come stumbling down the line.

Between the battered trenches their silent dead will lie
Quiet with grave eyes staring at the summer sky.
There is a mist upon them so that I cannot see
The faces of my friends that walk the little town with me.

Lest we see a worse thing than it is to die,
Live ourselves and see our friends cold beneath the sky,
God grant we too be lying there in wind and mud and rain
Before the broken regiments come stumbling back again.

             E. A. MACKINTOSH
     *1916, before the Somme battle*

## THE FORMATION OF A COMPANY

It was written that we should take part in the hatred that was to take place on the Somme; and to this end we marched southwards for many days.

Before the hatred began we went into trenches recently left by the French, and these same trenches were a rough house. The enemy blew up mines without number, so that the earth rocked like a sea, and the white craters of thrown-up chalk like the breaking of the waves. As the shells and mines descended from the sky, the men said 'This is worse than Ypres'.

But the sections did stout work, each after their fashion. The men of the West Country were unmoved when the Prussians came upon them; the Lancs men tunnelled and made emplacements; and the men of the Midlands did likewise. As for the Irish, we toiled not, neither did we spin, but fired our guns till none were left in action; and did the dirty work that remained with our rifles.

Thus were four sections joined into one Company.

*Journal: Machine Gun Corps*

THERE's a long, long raid a-coming
   Into the land of the Huns,
Where the Eau-de-C'logne is humming
   And where Krupps make guns.
It's a long, long time we've waited,
   And we've behaved far too well.
But now we're going to give those Germans
   What Lloyd George called—" Hell."

# A Winter's Night on the Somme.

## BRINGING UP THE BACON

Came the morn when he and I stopped short in
our tracks . . . an overnight ration-carrying party
had stopped a stray shell and now lay amid
scattered rations around the shell-crater. A familiar
enough sight, for every seasoned soldier knew the
possibility of precisely the same fate at any moment
and thus the period of our mourning was brief,
but pungent.

THEN . . . four eyes round as saucepan-lids were
riveted upon a large chunk of bacon, almost
hidden beneath the dead Sergeant's body.

Muddy and bloody, but BACON! Bacon . . . a
daily dream too seldom fulfilled, for the ration
was rare and too small at that; a tiny sliver: BUT
for those who had bread the added unspeakable
delight of a DIP in the the hot FAT!

One slavered at the thought that here was one
BIG LUMP of thick juicy slices and dozens of DIPS!

Yet I was assailed by a feeling of slight revulsion at
the thought of eating this blood-stained gift, but
Bernie yelped: "Blimey, wotsa droppa blood? It's
Sergeant's blood so it's all in the Army . . . come on,
let's 'urry up so we can get stuck into the food!"

Thus comforted I cancelled my objection and although
later soaking and scrubbing failed to lessen the large
stain we didn't even notice it after the first (secret)
meal.

It is a truism that when a man's empty stomach is
plastered up against his backbone there are few
arguments against eating, and no niceties will
intrude.

Thus I felt no cannibalistic stigma could exist and
became assured that this simple physical 'trans-
fusion' of Sergeant's blood had, by proxy as
it were, provided a spiritual promotion from the
anonymity of Private-Soldier to the height of
Non-Commissioned Rank.

*A. A. Payne*

He descended with unparalleled rapidity,
  His velocity 'twould beat me to compute
I speak with unimpeachable veracity,
  With evidence complete and absolute.
He suffered from spontaneous combustion
  As towards terrestrial sanctuary he dashe
And underwent complete disintegration,
  In other words—he crashed!

He straffed me with unmitigated violence,
  With wholly reprehensible abuse,
His language in its blasphemous simplicity
  Was rather more exotic than abstruse,
He mentioned that the height of his ambition
  Was to see your humble servant duly hung.
I returned to Home Establishment next morning,
  In other words—was stung!

## Carry On.

Tune : "Ten Little Nigger Boys."

Ten little bumble bees taking off in line,
One hit a sycamore, then there were nine.
Nine little bumble bees flying fast and straight,
One got a nasty bump, then there were eight.
Eight little bumble bees climbing up to heaven,
One struck an Archibald, then there were seven.
Seven little bumble bees attacking in a dive,
One met another one, then there were five.
Five little bumble bees way above the floor.
One saw the Hun machine, then there were four.
Four little bumble bees fighting fast and free,
One said his engine conked, and then there were three.
Three little bumble bees scrapping in the blue,
One came all over queer, and then there were two.
Two little bumble bees hiding in the sun,
One had a cross-feed jam, then there was one.
One little bumble bee, faint but still pursuing
He hasn't come back yet—nothing further doing.

My turns approximated to the vertical,
  I deemed it most judicious to proceed.
I frequently gyrated on my axis,
  And attained colossal atmospheric speed.
I descended with unparalleled momentum,
  My propeller's point of rupture I surpassed,
And performed the most astounding evolutions,
  In other words—split-arsed!

## COLLISION COURSE

For a fleeting instant of time I looked into the face of the observer and the cockpit in which he stood. He thought that I would hit him head on and wipe him from existence, torn to fragments with the whirring engine and propeller that I carried. So did I. For a fragment of time I hung in space, mentally, already dead. The observer and I saw each other as souls already hurled into the eternal cosmos.

There was but one thing to do.

'My God,' I breathed in prayer, even as I did it. I yanked the Camel's stick hard into my stomach and flashed between the two-seater's wings and tail plane as my gallant little Camel answered to the pull. By a miracle we missed collision, by a miracle my Camel held togehter. I flat spun upside down on top of a loop and fell out sideways. I had lost height so rapidly in my downward rush from 14,000 feet that the pressure in my fuel-tank had not had time to stabilize to meet the higher atmospheric pressure, and my engine ceased to run. Not certain of the cause I tried her on the gravity tank and she picked up. I turned west and scanned the sky. High overhead I saw planes pass between the mist and sky like goldfish in a bowl held up against a curtained window. Around me and on my level there was nothing to be seen, no aeroplanes, enemy or friendly, except the R.E. 8 fast disappearing westward in the mist, westward towards the lines. The triplane and the Camel both had vanished. The ground below was free from shell-holes, but indistinct on account of the mist. I climbed upward as I travelled west and found some Camels of the Squadron. Our patrol time was finished, and we returned to our aerodrome in formation. And as I went I cursed the damn-fool pilot of the British R.E. 8.

*Norman Macmillan*

## OVER THE LINES

We were flying in formation and we kept our ruddy station,
   Though the wind was trying hard to sweep the sky.
And we watched the puffs of powder, heard the Archies booming louder
   And we didn't need to stop to reason why.

With the German lines below us, and a gale that seemed to throw us
   Into nowhere, as it would a schoolboy's kite,
We went skimming through the ether always keeping close together
   And we felt the joy of battle grip us tight.

Then from out of the horizon which we kept our eager eyes on
   Swept the Fokkers in their deadly fan-wise dash.
Soon the Vickers guns were cracking and a couple started backing,
   Whilst a third was sent down in a flaming flash.

How we blessed our Bristol Fighters, as we closed in with the blighters
   And we zoomed and banked and raced them through the air.
We abandoned our formation, but we won the situation,
   Won it easily, with four machines to spare.

Then Archie burst around us, and the beggar nearly found us,
   But we dived towards our lines without delay,
And we finished gay and merry on a binge of gin and sherry,
   For we knew we'd lived to see another day.

### "We haven't got a hope in the morning"

Tune : "John Peel."

WHEN you soar into the air on a Sopwith scout,
And you're scrapping with a Hun and your gun cuts out,
Well, you stuff down your nose till your plugs fall out,
'Cos you haven't got a hope in the morning.

*Chorus*

   For a batman woke me from my bed,
   I'd had a thick night and a very sore head,
   And I said to myself, to myself I said,
   " Oh, we haven't got a hope in the morning ! "

So I went to the sheds and examined my gun,
Then my engine I tried to run ;
And the revs. that it gave were a thousand and one,
'Cos it hadn't got a hope in the morning.

   *Chorus*—For a batman, etc.

We were escorting Twenty-Two,
Hadn't a notion what to do,
So we shot down a Hun and an F.E. too,
'Cos they hadn't got a hope in the morning !

   *Chorus*—For a batman, etc.

We went to Cambrai, all in vain,
The F.E.'s said, " We must explain ;
Our cameras broke ; we must do it again ;
Oh, we haven't got a hope to-morrow morning.

   *Chorus*—For a batman, etc.

When the Fiend of War is sleeping,
 Glutted sleek with human prey,
And the setting sun is creeping
To the West, and shadows deepening
 From the shell-scarred tower of Ypres
 at the closing of the day.

When the peaceful sky is ringing
 With no hideous sound of strife,
And a skylark downward winging
Thrills the evening with his singing,
 His mellow anthem teeming with the
 ringing joy of life.

Then we dream of other places,
 Peaceful, too, that lie afar;
And the dream of other faces,
Other voices, soon effaces,
 All discordant thoughts and fancies,
 grim imaginings of War.

And we build the golden towers
 Upon Fancy's faery keep,
And we cull the magic flowers
In Imagination's bowers,
 As we roam the purple twilight where
 the twin-born spirits sleep.

And we wonder if those furrows,
 Reaching out on every hand,
Are in truth the haunts where burrows
Tiny Man, and where the heroes
 Nightly leave their clammy shelter,
 seeking death in No Man's Land

Brief our thought! For as we wonder
 The Fiend Monster, from his lair,
Feels his vitals gnawed asunder
By the Blood Lust. Then the thunder
 Of a battery sends its challenge
 shrieking shrilly through the air.

Then, with rancorous hell-hate screaming,
 Comes "Retaliation" back,
Through a sky, no longer seeming
One of peace, but devil-teeming,
 Which the hounds of hell are cleaving
 in a furied, maddened pack.

And the air is fouled with stenches—
 Mingled powder, blood and clay—
For each hidden monster belches
Ghastly death upon the trenches
 While the crimson sun is fleeing
 from his desecrated day.

All around are bursting flashes;
 Now and then a mighty flare
As a "heavy" salvo crashes
Where the Cloth Hall stands in ashes,
 Yellow through the sulphureous pall
 where bursts the "Woolly Bear."

Across No Man's Land is sweeping,
 Through the "Rapids" leaden rain,
Yelling khaki, crawling, leaping . . .
Grinning Death is reaping . . . reaping—
 What matter! If we win the trench
 His reaping is in vain!

And so the Monster rages
 Till his frothing, dripping jaw
In the recking blood assuages,
For a time, the gnawing stages
 Of the blood-thirst ever craving from
 his ever-gaping maw.

Then the pallid, twisted faces
 Of our dead on No Man's Land
Will remain the only traces
'Neath the quiet, starlit spaces,
 And we'll dream of other faces,
 dreaming sleeping as we stand.

J. H. O'K.

## SOUND OF MUSIC

In about May or June, 1916, I was in the trenches
in front of Gammercourt Wood, on the Somme.
I was in the First London Regiment, R.F., part
of the 56th London Division. The lines thereabouts
were a good distance apart and quite quiet,
during the lull before the murderous shelling
which opened the Somme attack on the 1st July.
We had heard organ music coming from Jerry's
lines during quiet spells at night, and the
locality of the organ was the subject of some
argument. In a dug-out, in Gammercourt church,
in a ruined house? We never did know.
One night I was on patrol with an officer and
another chap. We crept out and lay against Jerry's
wire, listening for working parties in his trenches
and support areas.

Then we heard quite clearly, only occasionally
interrupted by machine guns and shells passing
over, the organ commence playing.
It started with the usual highbrow and sacred
stuff and then suddenly switched to 'Somewhere
A Voice Is Calling' played through twice, and
then 'My Little Grey Home In The West' -
recognisable, but not so clear. It really sounded
marvellous in those surroundings.
We heard afterwards that one of the officers
in another unit had thrown some song sheets
into Jerry's trench, as nearly all the division heard
the organ at some time or another.

*Private Dobell, 4686,*
*1st City of London Regiment,*
*Royal Fusiliers.*

When you've landed in the country,
  And you're fed up with the train,
Don't think your troubles finished,
  For they will follow in a chain;
So keep your faces smiling
  When the billet meets your eye,
You all expected different,
  But to sleep you'll surely try.
When reveille breaks your slumber,
  To wash your thoughts will jump;
But no blessed water can you get,
  There's no handle on the pump.
But streams there are in plenty,
  So your Christian ways redeem;
But take care you don't fall in one—
  Things are not always what they seem.
If the language you go in for,
  It will play you funny pranks,
But the language most convincing
  Is the colour of five francs.
Then you patronise Estaminets,
  And you learn to drink the beer,
It has redeeming features,
  For it never makes you queer.
You will try to Parley-voo,
  With one and all you see,
And you get some nasty shocks,
  When they tell you: "Me no comprée."*
So you drop back on good old English,
  And swear like a Spanish Don,
Then smack your lips o'er the beer you drink,
  And say this, "Tres Bon."
When with rats and lice tormented,
  For the trenches you declare,
Don't think your troubles left behind,
  They'll follow everywhere.
So like the old Crusader,
  With a helmet on your head,
You march in full equipment,
  And wish the Kaiser dead.
On arrival in the trenches,
  Just keep your head down tight,
And remember that to show yourself
  Is asking for "Good-night."
When home no doubt you grumbled,
  If they hadn't made your bed,
But you'll be lucky in the dug-out
  To find a place to rest your head.
When walking through the trenches,
  You off the boards do slip;
Don't pretend you did it purposely,
  As you dearly loved a dip.
When you're out upon patrol work,
  And a flare lights up the sky,
Be sure to lie quite flat and still,
  Or for you young Fritz will try.
When you cook upon the brazier,
  And your pals come round to talk,
Don't let the captain catch you
  Using bayonet as toasting fork.
Your helmet, too, was issued
  From shrapnel fire to save you,

So don't think it is a saucepan,
  To be used for making "Gippo."†
When worn out with making gooseberries,
  And you wish it all in ——,
Don't curse the Sergt.-Major,
  If "Stand to" he has to yell.
Just the same with all your rations.
  When the bread is rather bare,
Don't curse the Quartermaster;
  Some day you'll have your share.
And when back again in billets,
  Although people may prove kind,
You'll ne'er see a damsel half so nice
  As the one you left behind.

* This is not the natives' pidgin English or Tommy's pidgin French, but a real sample of the atrocious French spoken by some of the peasants and villagers with whom our troops find themselves; also, it is not *patois*—that they speak fluently. "Me no allez" is also often heard. No grammar exists in the French of these people. You will often be addressed as follows: "Vois la la-bas boutique no bon l'autre tres bon, mademoiselle tres jolie."

† Soup, *ragout.*

*Gippo,* which comes from the Arabic, is merely one of many such words incorporated in Army parlance by the British Army' long association with the Orient. *Pozzi*—jam; *wallah*—as person; *pukkah*—proper, real, genuine, are a few of the commonest.

In this parody, as usual, the Sergeant-Major, food and girls form good topics for a rhyme.

## TAFAS

The village lay stilly under its slow wreaths of
white smoke, as we rode near, on our guard.
Some grey heaps seemed to hide in the long grass,
embracing the ground in the close way of corpses.
We looked away from these, knowing they were
dead; but from one a little figure tottered off, as
if to escape us. It was a child, three or four years
old, whose dirty smock was stained red over one
shoulder and side, with blood from a large half-
fibrous wound, perhaps a lance thrust, just where
neck and body joined.

The child ran a few steps, then stood and cried
to us in a tone of astonishing strength (all else
being very silent), 'Don't hit me, Baba.' Abd el
Aziz, choking out something—this was his village,
and she might be of his family—flung himself off
his camel, and stumbled, kneeling, in the grass
beside the child. His suddenness frightened her,
for she threw up her arms and tried to scream;
but, instead, dropped in a little heap, while the
blood rushed out again over her clothes; then, I
think, she died.

We rode past the other bodies of men and women
and four more dead babies, looking very soiled in
the daylight, towards the village; whose loneliness
we now knew meant death and horror. By the
outskirts were low mud walls, sheepfolds, and on
one something red and white. I looked close and
saw the body of a woman folded across it, bottom
upwards, nailed there by a saw bayonet whose haft
stuck hideously into the air from between her
naked legs. About her lay others, perhaps twenty
in all, variously killed.
The Zaagi burst into wild peals of laughter, the
more desolate for the warm sunshine and clear
air of this upland afternoon. I said, 'The best of
you brings me the most Turkish dead,' and we
turned after the fading enemy, on our way shooting
down those who had fallen out by the roadside and
came imploring our pity. One wounded Turk, half-
naked, not able to stand, sat and wept to us.
Abdulla turned away his camel's head, but the
Zaagi, with curses, crossed his track and whipped
three bullets from his automatic through the man's
bare chest. The blood came out with his heartbeats,
throb, throb, throb, slower and slower.

*T. E. Lawrence.*

### Untitled

All the hills and vales along
Earth is bursting into song,
And the singers are the chaps
Who are going to die perhaps.
    O sing, marching men,
    Till the valleys ring again.
    Give your gladness to earth's keeping,
    So be glad, when you are sleeping.

Cast away regret and rue,
Think what you are marching to,
Little give, great pass.
Jesus Christ and Barabbas
Were found the same day.
This died, that, went his way.
    So sing with joyful breath.
    For why, you are going to death.
    Teeming earth will surely store
    All the gladness that you pour.

Earth that never doubts nor fears
Earth that knows of death, not tears,
Earth that bore with joyful ease
Hemlock for Socrates,

Earth that blossomed and was glad
'Neath the cross that Christ had,
Shall rejoice and blossom too
When the bullet reaches you.
    Wherefore, men marching
    On the road to death, sing!
    Pour gladness on earth's head,
    So be merry, so be dead.

From the hills and valleys earth
Shouts back the sound of mirth,
Tramp of feet and lilt of song
Ringing all the road along.
All the music of their going,
Ringing swinging glad song-throwing,
Earth will echo still, when foot
Lies numb and voice mute.
    On marching men, on
    To the gates of death with song.
    Sow your gladness for earth's reaping,
    So you may be glad though sleeping.
    Strew your gladness on earth's bed,
    So be merry, so be dead.

C. H. SORLEY

# The Last Long Mile

THEY put us in the Army and they handed us a pack,
They took away our nice new clothes and dressed us up in kak,
They marched us twenty miles and more to fit us for the war,
We didn't mind the nineteen but the last one made us sore.

*Chorus*

Oh it's not the pack that you carry on your back
Nor the gun upon your shoulder,
Nor the five-inch crust of France's dirty dust
That makes you feel your limbs are growing older.
It's not the load on the hard straight road
That drives away your smile;
If the sox of sister raise a blister
Blame it on the last long mile.

One day we had manœuvres on dear old Salisbury Plain,
We marched and marched and marched and marched and marched and marched again.
I thought the Duke of York a fool but he wasn't in the van
With us who marched and marched and marched and marched back home again.

*Chorus*

Oh it's not the pack that you carry on your back
Nor the gun upon your shoulder,
If there's never any ham, there's plum and apple jam
To make you feel your limbs are growing older.
Oh it's not the camp, nor the echoes of the tramp
That drives away your smile,
It's the sergeant-major's little wager,
To beat you on the last long mile.

## WAR COURTSHIP AND MARRIAGE.

### Warning Against Lovers from Overseas.

Mr. J. B. Capper, St. Michael's, Reigate, writes to *The Times*:—

May I ask you to publish a warning to parents and guardians, and to marriageable girls themselves, based upon recent experience within my personal knowledge?

It is required not by reason of special depravity in any particular set of men, but because social conditions are profoundly affected by the war.

A young lady, well known to me, and highly and justly respected, was courted with every apparent circumstance of scrupulous honour by one who had volunteered, from another part of the world, to fight for the Allied cause.

Her family made every inquiry that seemed possible in the case of one whose home was far away, and the engagement was recognised, and had been made known, when—happily before it was too late—the fact came to light that the would-be bridegroom had a wife and child living in the land from which he came.

I have been begged to write this on behalf of the lady and her family, who are anxious to warn others of the risks that may be run it, owing to the difficulty of prosecuting at a distance such inquiries as would be thought indispensable in this country, proposals apparently honourable are too trustfully accepted.

It is usually possible at least to find out something about the next-of-kin of a fighting man, and, if he be serving in the ranks, to learn whether they are receiving the separation allowance.

**FIGHT THE GOOD FIGHT (1).**
FIGHT THE GOOD FIGHT WITH ALL THY MIGHT,
CHRIST IS THY STRENGTH, AND CHRIST
THY RIGHT;
LAY HOLD ON LIFE, AND IT SHALL BE
THY JOY AND CROWN ETERNALLY.
BAMFORTH. (Copyright)

**FIGHT THE GOOD FIGHT (3).**
CAST CARE ASIDE, LEAN ON THY GUIDE.
HIS BOUNDLESS MERCY WILL PROVIDE.
TRUST, AND THY TRUSTING SOUL SHALL PROVE.
CHRIST IS ITS LIFE, AND CHRIST ITS LOVE.
BAMFORTH. (Copyright)

**FIGHT THE GOOD FIGHT (2)**
RUN THE STRAIGHT RACE, THROUGH GOD'S
GOOD GRACE,
LIFT UP THINE EYES, AND SEEK HIS FACE;
LIFE WITH ITS WAY BEFORE THEE LIES,
CHRIST IS THE PATH, AND CHRIST THE PRIZE.
BAMFORTH. (Copyright).

**1**
If the Sergeant steals your rum,
　　Never mind!
If the Sergeant steals your rum,
　　Never mind!
Though he's just a noisy pot,
You can let him take the lot,
If the Sergeant steals your rum
　　Never mind!
**2**
When old Jerry shells your trench,
　　Never mind!
When old Jerry shells your trench,
　　Never mind!
Though the sandbags bust and fly
You have only once to die,
If old Jerry shells the trench,
　　Never mind!

**3**
If you get stuck on the wire,
　　Never mind!
If you get stuck on the wire,
　　Never mind!
Though you've stuck there all the day
They count you dead and stop your pay,
If you get stuck on the wire,
　　Never mind!

**4**
If the Sergeant says you're mad
　　Never mind!
P'haps you are a little bit,
　　Never mind!
Just be calm, don't answer back,
'Cos the Sergeant stands no 'slack',
So if he says you are mad,
　　Well—　you are.

## LES SOLDATS ANGLAIS

This is the way the battalions came

Steadily, steadily over the hill;

This is the way the horse guns came;

And if you listen you'll hear them still;

The ghosts, the ghosts, of long dead hosts

The whispers of Saxons in silent throats;

They flit through the salient in soundless hosts,

Those long dead soldiers from the British coast.


Some Belgian child who cannot sleep

Whispers to mother of 'marching feet':

Les soldats Anglais, ma chére petite

Their ghosts, their ghosts,

Les soldats Anglais; their sleepless ghosts.

*C. W. Archer*

### The Aisne

We saw fire on the tragic slopes
Where the flood-tide of France's early gain,
Big with wrecked promise and abandoned hopes,
Broke in a surf of blood along the Aisne.

The charge her heroes left us, we assumed,
What, dying, they reconquered, we preserved,
In the chill trenches, harried, shelled, entombed,
Winter came down on us, but no man swerved.

Winter came down on us. The low clouds, torn
In the stark branches of the riven pines,
Blurred the white rockets that from dusk till morn
Traced the wide curve of the close-grappling lines.

In rain, and fog that on the withered hill
Froze before dawn, the lurking foe drew down;
Or light snows fell that made forlorner still
The ravaged country and the ruined town;

Or the long clouds would end. Intensely fair,
The winter constellations blazing forth –
Pursues, the Twins, Orion, the Great Bear –
Gleamed on our bayonets pointing to the north.

There where, firm links in the unyielding chain,
Where fell the long-planned blow and fell in vain –
Hearts worthy of the honour and the trial,
We helped to hold the lines along the Aisne.

ALAN SEEGER

89

## Germany's Last Reserves: The Goose-Step at Hagenbeck's Zoo.

SKIBOO.
TUNE: Special.

Two German officers crossed the Rhine, Skiboo, Skiboo.
Two German officers crossed the Rhine, Skiboo, Skiboo.
 These German officers crossed the Rhine
 To love the women and taste the wine.
Skiboo, Skiboo, Skiboodley boo, Skidam, dam, dam.

1915 — Grenadier Guard.　　　Gordon Highlander Piper.　　　R.F.A.　　　Flying Corps.

# Flack & Sons
## Military Boot Makers,
## 9, Bridge Street,
### CAMBRIDGE.

Professor Hughes having a Pair of Messrs. Flack & Sons boots on carries his friend Von-Zittel across the Hot Stream flowing from the Giant Geyser, as he had on only a pair made in Germany.

They came to an inn on top of a rise, Skiboo, Skiboo,
A famous French inn of stupendous size, Skiboo, Skiboo,
  They saw a maiden all dimples and sighs,
  The two together said " Damn her eyes."
Skiboo, Skiboo, Skiboodley boo, Skidam, dam, dam.

Oh, landlord, you've a daughter fair, Skiboo, Skiboo,
Oh, landlord, you've a daughter fair, Skiboo, Skiboo.
  Oh, landlord, you've a daughter fair,
  With lily-white arms and golden hair.
Skiboo, Skiboo, Skiboodley boo, Skidam, dam, dam.

Nein, nein, mein Herr, she's far too young, Skiboo, Skiboo,
Nein, nein, mein Herr, she's far too young, Skiboo Skiboo.
  *Mais non, mon pere*, I'm not so young—
  I've often been kissed by the farmer's son.
Skiboo, Skiboo, Skiboodley boo, Skidam, dam, dam.

The rest of the tale I can't relate, Skiboo, Skiboo,
For tho' it's old, it's up to date, Skiboo, Skiboo.
  The story of man seducing a maid
  Is not for you—you're too sedate.
Skiboo, Skiboo, Skiboodley boo, Skidam, dam, dam

   A well-purged and diminutive version of a famous heirloom of the British Army ; in its original state consists of about forty verses.

*Irish Rifle.*    *1st Life Guard.*    *Seaforth Highlander.*       *Staff Officer.*       *R.A.M.C.*    *Army Service Corps.*

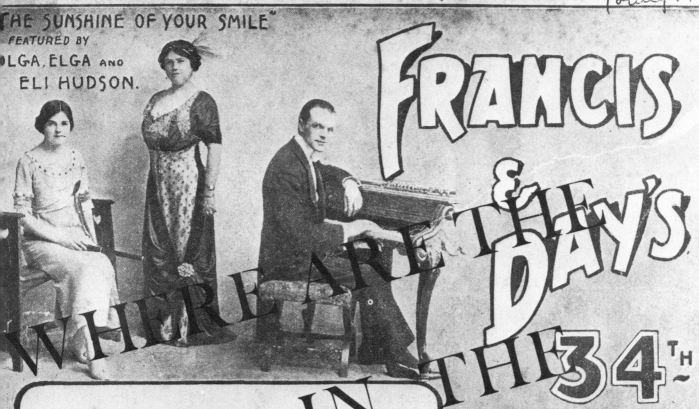

"THE SUNSHINE OF YOUR SMILE"
FEATURED BY
OLGA, ELGA AND ELI HUDSON.

# FRANCIS & THE DAY'S 34TH ANNUAL

WITH TONIC SOL-FA SETTING.

## CONTENTS.

The Sunshine of your Smile. *Ballad*
Olga, Elga & Eli Hudson
Sister Susie's sewing shirts for soldiers   Jack Norworth
Here we are! Here we are!! Here we are again!!!
Mark Sheridan
Where are the lads of the Village to-night?
George Lashwood
Never mind!   ...   ...   ...   *Miss Gertie Gitana*
Wee hoose 'mang the Heather   ...   ...   Harry Lauder
I was a good little girl till I met you   Miss Clarice Mayne
Gilbert the Filbert   ...   "The Passing Show" Revue
I'll make a man of you...   "The Passing Show" Revue
Kitty, the Telephone Girl   ...   "Hullo, Tango!" Revue
We're really proud of you   ...   ...   Miss Ellaline Terriss
Now, are we all here?   Yes!   ...   ...   Whit Cunliffe
The Army of to-day's all right   ...   Miss Vesta Tilley
Waiting   ...   ...   ...   ...   ...   G. H. Elliott
My Boy. *Ballad*   Florence Smithson and Emily Hayes
Row me on the River, Romeo   "A Year in an Hour" Revue
Belgium put the "kibosh" on the Kaiser   Mark Sheridan
That was the end of my dream   ...   Miss Evie Greene
Oh! to-morrow night ...   ...   ...   S. W. Wyndham
Johnny O'Morgan on his Little Mouth Organ,
      Playing "Home, Sweet Home"   ...   Miss Lily Lena
Why do they call me Archibald?   ...   ...   Jack Pleasants
I've been out with Johnny Walker ...   Miss Hetty King
I followed her here and I followed her there   Whit Cunliffe
Make me the king of your heart. *Ballad*   Walter Williams

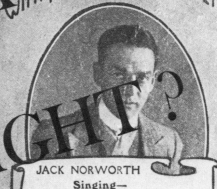

JACK NORWORTH
Singing—
"Sister Susie's sewing shirts
for Soldiers."

LONDON:
FRANCIS, DAY & HUNTER,
138-140, CHARING CROSS ROAD.

NEW YORK: T. B. HARMS & FRANCIS, DAY & HUNTER, 62-64, WEST 45th STREET.

# WHERE ARE THE LADS OF THE VILLAGE TO-NIGHT?

WRITTEN BY R. P. WESTON.

COMPOSED BY H. E. DAREWSKI.

SUNG BY GEORGE LASHWOOD.

bar - maid at you tries to wink, but with a tear - drop has to blink, And won't be a
Per - cy, tho' at sea a lot, is not at Cowes up - on his yacht; When last our
all the boys are do - ing grand for King and Home and Mo - ther - land, And when at

shamed to tell you why.................... Tho' the mob their flags are wag - ging, sing - ing
"Per - cy boy" was seen.................... He was back as mas - ter gun - ner on a
last they've turn'd the tide,.................... Tho' Ber lin's the place they'll rush for, they'll do

Jin - go songs and brag - ging, All the girls will ask each oth - er with a sigh....................
twen - ty thou - sand ton - ner, Drop - ping shells up - on a Ger - man sub - ma - rine....................
noth - ing we need blush for, No, they'll play the game, and we shall say with pride....................

CHORUS. *2nd time f.*

Where are the lads of the Vil - lage to - night? Where are the "nuts" we knew?....................

In Pic - ca - dil - ly? in Leices - ter Square? No, not there!

No, not there! They're tak - ing a trip on the Con - ti - nong With their ri - fles and their

bay - 'nets bright,...............
1. Fac - ing dan - ger glad - ly where they're need - ed bad - ly,
2. Gone to teach the Vul - ture mur - der is not cul - ture,
3. Where the Kai - ser, hum - bled, knows his pow'r has crum - bled,

That's where they are to - night!........................ - night!........................

1st time.

2nd time.

D.C.

## ODE TO TICKLER.*

TUNE: "*Sweet Genevieve.*"

Oh, jam for tea! Oh, jam for tea,
I'm jolly sure it don't suit me;
I've tried for years, and now in tears,
I'll sing it to you mournfully.

Oh, jam for tea! Oh, jam for tea!
The world knows how you've tortured me;
I've frills and squills, you've made me bills,
And filled the dentists' empty tills.

Oh, jam for tea! Oh, jam for tea!
Fried bully† and Maconochie;‡
But when we get back to Blighte-e-e-e....
We will have ham and lamb for tea.

\* Jam maker to the Army.
† Bully beef—otherwise corned beef.
‡ The maker's name: a tinned food issued to Tommy, con-
sting usually of tinned tomatoes, haricots, potatoes, some sort
meat, usually fat, and some shiny stuff that might be gravy
jelly.

## Plum and Apple

ung to the tune of "*A Wee Deoch an' Doris*"

Plum and Apple,
Apple and Plum,
Plum and Apple,
There is always some
The A.S.C. get strawberry jam
And lashings of rum,
But we poor blokes
We only get—
Apple and Plum.

# The Eternal Question.

"When the 'ell is it goin' to be strawberry?"

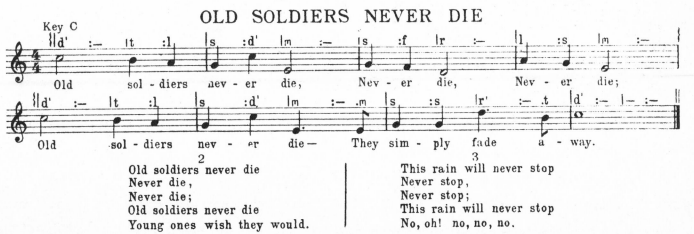

# OLD SOLDIERS NEVER DIE

Key C

Old sol-diers nev-er die, Nev-er die, Nev-er die;
Old sol-diers nev-er die— They sim-ply fade a-way.

**2**
Old soldiers never die
Never die,
Never die;
Old soldiers never die
Young ones wish they would.

**3**
This rain will never stop
Never stop,
Never stop;
This rain will never stop
No, oh! no, no, no.

*Infantry Office, Hounslow.* 15/1/1916.

Sir,

I regret to inform you that ——, 11th Battn. Middlesex Regt., G.S., is ill at 38th Field Ambulance, France, suffering from wounds and shock (mine explosion).

*1st January,* 1916.

Dear Mother,

I am very sorry I did not write before now, but we were in the trenches on Christmas Day and we had a lot to do. Also I was sent to the hospital. I am feeling a little better, so don't get upset. Don't send any letters to the company, because I won't get them. Also you cannot send any letters to the hospital, as I won't get them. Dear Mother, do not worry, I will be all right. Hoping all of you are getting on well. I was only hurt in the back. I will try to send you letters every few days, to let you know how I am getting on. We get plenty of food in the hospital. Dear Mother, I know it will break your heart this, but don't get upset about it. I will be all right, but I would very much like to see you . . .

*6th January,* 1916.

. . . I have been in hospital nine days, lying in bed all the time, and now I have a sore heel . . . I had it cut and it is getting on better . . .

*20th January,* 1916.

Dear Mother, I am quite well and I came out of hospital on Wednesday (19th).

*24th January,* 1916.

. . . Dear Mother, you don't know how I was longing for a letter from you! I would like to know what the War Office said was the matter with me.

*26th January,* 1916.

. . . I am sending this photo of one of the officers who was killed . . . . He was very good to us . . . . Please frame it for a keepsake . . . .

Dear Mother, I have sent you a letter that I have received the parcel. I am well, hoping all of you are quite well.

Dear Mother, we were in the trenches and I was ill, so I went out and they took me to the prison and I am in a bit of trouble now, and won't get any money for a long time. I will have to go in front of a Court. I will try my best to get out of it, so don't worry. But, dear Mother, try to send some money, not very much, but try your best. I will let you know in my next how I get on. Give my best love to Father, and Kate.

From your loving son,
Aby.

Sir,

I am directed to inform you that a report has been received from the War Office to the effect that No. ——, 11th Battn. Middlesex Regiment, G.S., was sentenced after trial by court martial to suffer death by being shot for desertion, and the sentence was duly executed on 20th March, 1916.

I am, Sir, your obedient servant,
P. G. Hendley, 2nd Lieut.,
for Colonel I.C. Infantry Records.

Hounslow, *8th April,* 1916.

*Sylvia Pankhurst*

## The Deserter

'I'm sorry I done it, Major.'
We bandaged the livid face;
And led him out, ere the wan sun rose,
To die his death of disgrace.

The bolt-heads locked to the cartridge;
The rifles steadied to rest,
As cold stock nestled at colder cheek
And foresight lined on the breast.

'*Fire!*' called the Sergeant-Major.
The muzzles flamed as he spoke:
And the shameless soul of a nameless man
Went up in the cordite-smoke.

GILBERT FRANKAU

## THEY ALSO SERVE

*12th Sept.* General de Maud'huy had just been roused from sleep on the straw of a shed and was standing in the street, when a little group of unmistakable purport came round the corner. Twelve soldiers and an N.C.O., a firing party, a couple of gendarmes, and between them an unarmed soldier. My heart sank and a feeling of horror overcame me. An execution was about to take place. General de Maud'huy gave a look, then held up his hand so that the party halted, and with his characteristic quick step went up to the doomed man. He asked what he had been condemned for. It was for abandoning his post. The General then began to talk to the man. Quite simply he explained discipline to him. Abandoning your post was letting down your pals, more, it was letting down your country that looked to you to defend her. He spoke of the necessity of example, how some could do their duty without prompting but others, less strong, had to know and understand the supreme cost of failure. He told the condemned man that his crime was not venial, not low, and that he must die as an example, so that others should not fail. Surprisingly the wretch agreed, nodded his head. The burden of infamy was lifted from his shoulders. He saw a glimmer of something, redemption in his own eyes, a real hope, though he knew he was to die.

Maud'huy went on, carrying the man with him to comprehension that any sacrifice was worth while if it helped France ever so little. What did anything matter if he knew this?

Finally de Maud'huy held out his hand: 'Yours also is a way of dying for France,' he said. The procession started again, but now the victim was a willing one. The sound of a volley in the distance announced that all was over. General de Maud'huy wiped the beads of perspiration from his brow, and for the first time perhaps his hand trembled as he lit his pipe.

*E. L. Spears*

SHOT FOR SELLING INFORMATION TO THE GERMANS: A FRENCH TRAITOR. This unhappy French soldier was bribed by the Germans, for a hundred francs, to signal to them the position of the French guns near Rheims. Thus he sold the lives of his comrades, so to speak, fo "thirty pieces of (German) silver." He paid the penalty for his treachery with his life: but was i: not a greater crime to tempt him?—[*Photo. by Topical*]

## WEIGHTED SCALES

*14th Sept.* I had a conversation with one of the officers connected with the court martial that condemned these people, and shudderingly remarked that the evidence was slight, the accusation often improbable, and how could guilt be established in such cases without the possibility of error? His answer made a profound impression on me. 'You English don't know what war is. The existence of France is at stake. A single spy may cause such harm as to imperil the fate of the nation. Justice has little to do with it. Our duty is to see that no spy escapes whatever the cost may be. If a proportion of those who are executed to-day are guilty, even one or two, we have every reason to be satisfied that our duty to the country has been done.

*E. L. Spears*

99

# Unfortunately 'C' Coy gives a Concert!

Tom Green

The 'Queries'

## THE NEW WEAPON

Inside, above the noise of the engine, was heard the sharp cracking of our own machine-guns, mingled with the groaning and whining of the gunner who lay stretched along the blood and oil-saturated floor; this, with the vomiting of our second driver, intense heat, exhaust petrol fumes, and nauseous vapour from the guns made an inferno that no outside observer would have thought possible to exist within those steel plates. . . .

We lay under cover of the tank for the next five hours, during which the tank was repeatedly shelled by the Germans in the hope of totally destroying it, these shells falling all around, sometimes spraying us with earth and small stones. We were momentarily in expectation of one dropping amongst us, making a finish once and for all.

Hour after hour we watched for the promised assistance, but in vain; not a man saw we during that interminable afternoon. We were in "No Man's Land"; the ceaseless click, click of German machine-guns from the village was plainly heard; overhead aeroplane combatants could be seen fighting with their guns, but out fighting was done. There we lay, like many thousands of other poor soldiers stricken on the field, hoping against hope for the help which never came.

*Arthur Jenkin*

## TANK CHARGE

The immediate onset of the tanks inevitably was overwhelming. The German outposts, dazed or annihilated by the sudden deluge of shells, were overrun in an instant. The triple belts of wire were crossed as if they had been beds of nettles, and 350 pathways were sheared through them for the infantry. The defenders of the front trench, scrambling out of dug-outs and shelters to meet the crash and flame of the barrage, saw the leading tanks almost upon them, their appearance made the more grotesque and terrifying by the huge black bundles they carried on their cabs. As these tanks swung left-handed and fired down into the trench, others also surmounted by these appalling objects, appeared in multitudes behind them out of the mist. It is small wonder that the front Hindenburg Line, that fabulous excavation which was to be the bulwark of Germany, gave little trouble.

*D. G. Browne*

## ORGANISED CHAOS

We were in a field near Ypres, the French gunners with their field guns were blazing away with their 75's like hell let loose, bikes were forgotten for the time being and we were doled out with more ammunition and with the officer in charge made for St. Julian. This part was occupied by the Canadian Scottish, but they had taken a hell of a battering. There were a number of them in an old bar, most of them were wounded and in bad shape and crying out for water. We could do nothing, but one of our men was sent back to St. Jeanne to inform the R.A.M.C. in the advanced dressing station, and I heard somebody eventually arrived with water and got most of the bad cases away. Things were pretty hot around this quarter by now; for three days and nights we were blazing away all mixed up in different units, being ordered by different officers to go here and there — it was a real do. Eventually we were relieved and a few of us wandered back to our field which contained plenty of shell holes since we were last there.

We had 48 hours of hell when, during the third night, the tramp of feet mingled with the sound of Jerry machine gun fire and the relief had arrived; three of us made our way back to the field, starved but couldn't find anybody. We got down to it under a hedge and managed to sleep in short doses. When day broke we searched around and found some of ours digging in the woods close by, and throughout the day in whispers — Where's old so and so — I am afraid that was going to be the cry for all time. If Jerry had only known what was in front of him he could have gone wherever he liked without any opposition, but it was not to be, thank God.

*from Tom Green's Journal*

"BRINGING UP" THE RATIONS.
WINNING THE WAR SERIES:- No 7

## JUST BEFORE THE BATTLE, MOTHER (1).

Just before the battle, Mother, I am thinking most of you,
While upon the field we're watching, with the enemy in view.
Comrades brave are round me lying, fill'd with thoughts of friends
and home,
For well they know that on the morrow some will sleep beneath
the tomb.

BAMFORTH (Copyright).

## JUST BEFORE THE BATTLE, MOTHER (2).

Farewell, Mother, you may never, you may never, Mother,
Press me to your heart again;
But oh, you'll not forget me, Mother, you will not forget me,
If I'm number'd with the slain.

BAMFORTH (Copyright).

A REMARKABLE STORY OF FATHER AND SON
Captain E. W. Bowyer-Bower, R.F.C. (left), was shot down
above the Hindenburg Line, and his dead body was found by
his father, Captain T. Bowyer-Bower, R.E. (right).

## THE CASUALTIES.

The losses during these three days' fighting
were, I regret to say, very severe, numbering—

190 officers and 2,337 other ranks, killed,

359 officers and 8,174 other ranks, wounded,

23 officers and 1,728 other ranks, missing.

But the results attained were, in my opinion,
wide and far-reaching.

The enemy left several thousand dead on the
battlefield which were seen and counted; and
we have positive information that upwards of
12,000 wounded were removed to the north-
east and east by train.

Thirty officers and 1,657 other ranks of the
enemy were captured.

I can best express my estimate of this battle
by quoting an extract from a Special Order of
the Day which I addressed to Sir Douglas Haig
and the First Army at its conclusion:—

"I am anxious to express to you person-
ally my warmest appreciation of the skilful
manner in which you have carried out your
orders, and my fervent and most heartfelt
appreciation of the magnificent gallantry
and devoted, tenacious courage displayed by
all ranks whom you have ably led to success
and victory."

## JUST BEFORE THE BATTLE, MOTHER (3).

Oh, I long to see you, Mother, and the loving ones at
home,
But I'll never leave our banner till in honour I can come.
Tell the traitors all around you that their cruel words we
know,
In ev'ry battle kill our soldiers, by the help they give the
foe.

BAMFORTH (Copyright).

## THE FORTRESS OF ILE D'YEU

When a man has lost everything, and his life
hangs by no more than a hair, he watches over
it with an aching anxiety that he never had
for the riches of his former life. I had nothing
left but the empty, beastly inaction of my
fourth year in imprisonment—the mattress
in the casemate, the daily turnips, the ever-
dwindling bread ration—yet I clung to it with
a wild, instinctive stubbornness, watched
over it restlessly that my consciousness
should not slip from it, for if it once left
that fragment nothing else could follow but
an endless, dark wandering in madness.

On the morning after that night, and every
morning after it, I got up glad only to hear the
bugle, glad of the thin coffee and the watery,
tasteless vegetables, glad to see the soldiers'
bayonets, and if in those heavily passing
hours and days I felt consciousness again
trying to leave me I ran out into the yard,
trod out the counted steps of my walk, shut
my eyes, ears, spirit to the vertigo of
temptation, and blind and deaf and thought-
less ran and ran till I had left the haunting
behind me and nothing was left but the
life of a prisoner. I could not read any more,
for I was afraid of memories and dreamings.
It was always a dangerous bridge on which
the imagination slipped across to
frightening paths. There only remained the
cold water, the walks, the talk and the
cards and the chess and the meals and
sometimes the beastly unconsciousness of
drink. And even then it often happened that
I would spring up in the middle of cards or
talking and have to run out into the yard
because I thought I was going mad . . . .

The number of serious nerve cases increased
in that fourth winter. Two Germans went
raving mad. They were taken to a French
lunatic asylum, and there they died. The
other cases were only wrecks, but
apparently there was enough life in them
to prevent them being sent home.

*Aladar Kuncz*

## GRIM FOREBODING

The British sick were lying scattered amongst the
French and the Russians, both in the compound
No. 8 and in the other compounds of the camp.
Being sometimes dressed in French, Belgian, or
Russian uniforms, they were difficult to recognize.
They were lying in their clothes on the floor, or on
the straw mattresses above described. In the
beginning there were no beds in compound No. 8;
there were not even, as has been shown, mattresses
for all. Major Priestley saw delirious men waving
arms brown to the elbow with faecal matter. The
patients were alive with vermin; in the half light
he attempted to brush what he took to be an
accumulation of dust from the folds of a patient's
clothes, and he discovered it to be a moving mass
of lice. In one room in compound No. 8 the patients
lay so close to one another on the floor that he
had to stand straddle-legged across them to
examine them.

Captain Vidal's description is even more appalling.
It was impossible, he says, to obtain bedpans for the

British patients, and consequently in cases of delirium, and even in less serious cases, the state of the mattress was indescribable. Even such a thing as paper for sanitary purposes was almost unprocurable.

On one occasion only during the whole course of the epidemic did Dr. Aschenbach enter the hospital, or even the camp. His visit took place about four weeks after Major Priestley's arrival, and after some kind of order had been evolved. He came attired in a complete suit of protective clothing, including a mask and rubber gloves. His inspection was brief and rapid.

For his services in combating the epidemic, Dr. Aschenbach, the Committee understand, has been awarded the Iron Cross.

The cruelty of the administration at Wittenberg Camp from the very commencement has become notorious. Savage dogs were habitually employed to terrorize prisoners; flogging with a rubber whip was frequent. Men were struck with little or no provocation, and were tied to posts with their arms above their heads for hours. Captain Lauder reports that many of these men went so far as to look upon the typhus, with all its horrors, as a godsend; they preferred it to the presence of the German guards.

And the callousness during the outbreak even of so prominent an officer as Dr. Aschenbach as illustrated by an incident related by Captain Lauder. Shortly after their arrival at the camp, Major Fry, with Captain Lauder, was begging Dr. Aschenbach, standing outside the entanglements, for some medical requisite urgently required. One of his staff with Dr. Aschenbach was apparently favourably inclined towards the request, but it was curtly refused by Dr. Aschenbach, who turned away with the words "Schweine Englander."

*Parliamentary Paper (Report on the Prison Camp at Wittenburg)*

BLUE EYES (1).

Heart o' my dreams, in your face gleams
A light that has shown me the way
Into your heart, never to part,
Haunting me night and by day.

BLUE EYES (2).

Blue eyes, true eyes, sweetest I ever knew,
Blue eyes, true eyes, without them what should I do?
Someday love may fade like the June rose that dies,
But I'll keep on loving for ever and ever those two blue eyes.

# THE GAS ATROCITY IN FLANDERS.

## SUFFERINGS OF HILL 60 VICTIMS.

## THE SECRET PREPARATION OF THE POISON IN

## THE GERMAN CHEMICAL WORKS.

Sir John French has reported that those of the victims of the German gas poison who do not succumb on the field suffer acutely and, in a large proportion of cases, die a painful and lingering death, while those who survive will be invalids for life. The following extracts from a letter written by a British officer at the front speak of the terrible suffering of soldiers who were "gassed" during the German assaults on Hill 60.

Yesterday and the day before I went with —— to see some of the men in hospital at —— who were "gassed" yesterday and the day before on Hill 60. The whole of England and the civilised world ought to have the truth fully brought before them in vivid detail, and not wrapped up, as at present. When we got to the hospital we had no difficulty in finding out in which ward the men were, as the noise of the poor devils trying to get breath was sufficient to direct us. We were met by a doctor belonging to our division who took us into the ward. There were about twenty of the worst cases in the ward on mattresses, all more or less in a sitting position, propped up against the walls. Their faces, arms, and hands were of a shiny grey-black colour, mouth open and lead-glazed eyes; all swaying slightly backwards and forwards trying to get breath. It was the most appalling sight, all those poor black faces struggling for life. What with the groaning and the noise of the efforts for breath, Colonel ——, who, as everybody knows, has had as wide an experience as anyone all over the savage parts of Africa, told me to-day that he never felt so sick as he did after the scene.

In these cases there is practically nothing to be done for them, except to give them salt and water to try to make them sick. The effect the gas has is to fill the lungs with a watery, frothy matter, which gradually increases till it fills up the whole lungs and comes up to the mouth: then they die. It is suffocation—slow drowning,—taking, in some cases, one or two days. Eight died last night out of the twenty I saw, and most of the others I saw will die, while those who get over the gas invariably develop acute pneumonia.

It is, without doubt, the most awful form of scientific torture. Not one of the men I saw in hospital had a scratch or wound. The nurses and doctors were all working their utmost against this terror, but one could see from the tension of their nerves that it was like fighting a hidden danger which was overtaking everyone.

A German prisoner was caught with a respirator in his pocket. The pad was analysed, and found to contain hypo-sulphite of soda with 1 per cent of some other substance. The gas is in a cylinder, from which, when they send it out, it is propelled a distance of 100 yards. It then spreads. English people, men and women, ought to know exactly what is going on.

men, which was made of woollen material with spaces for the eyes, the cotton waste inside being saturated by the same solution. Dr. Haldane has again gone to the front to conduct experiments with various materials and methods.

**FASHIONS AT THE FRONT: THE GAS MASK.**—A photograph of an up-to-date gas mask and its adjuncts at the Exhibition of Canadian Official Photographs, Grafton Galleries, Grafton-street, W. 1.

## THE REASON WHY.

TUNE: "*Auld Lang Syne.*"

We're here because we're here,
Because we're here Because we're here
We're here because we're here,
Because we're here, Because we're here
Oh, here we are, oh, here we are,
Oh, here we are again.
Oh, here we are, oh, here we are,
Oh, here we are again.

AND SO ON, until exhausted.

# TOO MUCH GAS

I'd got my pass in the afternoon of August 4th, the anniversary of the War. I laid in the dugout praying nothing would happen until I was safely in the train. It did not. Straight from the line to the train couldn't be true. I think it was only a short leave at that time, 5 days, I'm almost certain. This kind of joy only comes once in a lifetime, never had its equal since.

Arrived home, my father had joined up, also my youngest brother. I couldn't sleep through the noise of the trams running all night along the Harrow Road. I spent my nights at the Coffee Stall at the bottom of our street. It was nice to see my mum and my sisters. The return journey was a nightmare, the old men doing home service holding hands with tears streaming down their faces holding back the relations who had come to Victoria to see the menfolk off to France. The returning leave crowd were very small in comparison.

The front at the Ypres Sector was shaped like a horse shoe. The Germans occupied the outside and had full command of all transport and supplies arriving for the front, so you can bet not much got through. I remember one morning after a very heavy bombardment seeing troops running back from the front line in red trousers. This shook us a bit as we had not seen them before. They were trying to speak to us and were holding bits of old rag to their mouths, then suddenly we realised what it was. The smell was very strong. We had an interpreter attached to us; I managed to find him and he spoke to one of the soldiers, darkies they were, and then he explained they were French Algerian troops and they had got the full force of the first gas attack. The gas clouds were getting near us by this time, so rag was the only thing useful at that period. Lumps of shirt were torn off, anywhere most handy, and dipped in water and tied around the mouth. If there were anybody who wasn't dead scared, let him come and tell me. They came back in droves; I didn't think there could have been any more of our side left in the front line. Everybody that could be got hold of was pounced upon, cooks, staff blokes, the lot, we were marched up the line to try and hold Jerry back, and did it stink — the smell of gas hung about for weeks.

*from Tom Green's Journal*

SIR OR MADAM,

I regret to have to inform you that a report has been received from the War Office to the effect that (No.) 32652H (3922) *late*

(Rank) Sgt. (Name) Burlton, A. A.

(Regiment) 1st Cambs. Regt.

has been wounded, and was admitted to 22nd General Hospital, Dannes Camières, France.

on the 17th day of July, 1917. The nature of the wound is Gassed (Shell) Severe.

I am to express to you the sympathy and regret of the Army Council.

**Any further information received in this office as to his condition will be at once notified to you.**

## CHRISTMAS DAY 1916

A commanding officer in his book 'History of 1st Battalion S.L.1. 1916-1918' wrote "Much apprehension was felt by the Higher Command that the Germans would attempt to bring about a Christmas fraternization. To discourage any such intentions, our artillery carried out a heavy bombardment during the day: this had the desired effect and only drew slight retaliation." This I believe to be the understatement of the century. 'Jerry' came over unarmed to fraternize - there were no trenches because of the terrible conditions, just isolated 'funk holes'. When they appeared, I as the Company Signaller and having been given a clear line through to Artillery H.Q., reported their appearance - and they were heavily straffed.

Ho! the War Lords did not want to risk having war hatred abated. Good God, the 'gun fodder' may have stopped the war and what occupation could be found for our Gallant Boys holed up in the War Office?

On the Somme in 1916 our Christmas dinner was Australian rabbit, frozen very hard. It was the devil of a job to skin, but we did enjoy it.
*L. T.*

There was a hard frost at Passchanedaele, and we had only biscuits and some bully for Christmas. I got a jar of mustard pickles from the haversack of a dead man to spread on the biscuits. It was like dining at the Ritz.
*J. B.*

## Far from Ypres I long to be

Sung to the tune of "*Sing me to Sleep*".

> Far, far from Ypres I long to be,
> Where German snipers can't get at me
> Damp is my dug-out,
> Cold are my feet,
> Waiting for whizz-bangs
> To send me to sleep.

## A DAY OFF

*25th Dec.* At 8.30 a.m. I was looking out, and saw four Germans leave their trenches and come towards us; I told two of my men to go and meet them, *unarmed* (as the Germans were unarmed), and to see that they did not pass the half-way line. We were 350—400 yards apart at this point. My fellows were not very keen, not knowing what was up, so I went out alone, and met Barry, one of our ensigns, also coming out from another part of the line. By the time we got to them, they were three quarters of the way over, and much too near our barbed wire, so I moved them back. There were three private soldiers and a stratcher-bearer, and their spokesman started off by saying that he thought it only right to come over and wish us a happy Christmas, and trusted us implicitly to keep the truce. He came from Suffolk, where he had left his best girl and a 3½ h.p. motor-bike! He told me that he could not get a letter to the girl, and wanted to send one through me. I made him write out a post card in front of me, in English, and I sent it off that night. I told him that she probably would not be a bit keen to see him again. We then entered on a long discussion on every sort of thing. I was dressed in an old stocking-cap and a man's overcoat, and they took me for a corporal, a thing which I did not discourage, as I had an eye to going as near their lines as possible. I asked them what orders they had from their officers as to coming over to us, and they said *none*; they had just come over out of goodwill . . . .

On my return at 10 a.m. I was surprised to hear a hell of a din going on, and not a single man left in my trenches; they were completely denuded (against my orders), and nothing lived! I heard strains of *Tipperary* floating down the breeze, swiftly followed by a tremendous burst of *Deutschland uber Alles*, and as I got to my own Coy. H.-qrs. dug-out, I saw, to my

## The Point of View
" Well, if it don't get merrier than this by Christmas, it won't be up to much "

109

amazement, not only a crowd of about 150 British and Germans at the half-way house which I had appointed opposite my lines, but six or seven such crowds, all the way down our lines, extending towards the 8th Division on our right. I bustled out and asked if there were any German officers in my crowd, and the noise died down (as this time I was myself in my own cap and badges of rank).

I found two, but had to talk to them through an interpreter, as they could neither talk English nor French . . . I explained to them that strict orders must be maintained as to meeting half-way, and everyone unarmed; and we both agreed not to fire until the other did, thereby creating a complete deadlock and armistice (if strictly observed) . . . .

Meanwhile Scots and Huns were fraternizing in the most genuine possible manner. Every sort of souvenir was exchanged, addresses given and received, photos of families shown, etc. One of our fellows offered a German a cigarette; the German said, 'Virginian?' Our fellow said, 'Aye, straight-cut': the German said, 'No thanks, I only smoke Turkish!' (Sort of 10/- a 100 to me!) It gave us all a good laugh.

A German N.C.O. with the Iron Cross—gained, he told me, for conspicuous skill in sniping—started his fellows off on some marching tune. When they had done I set the note for *"The Boys of Bonnie Scotland, where the heather and the bluebells grow,"* and so we went on, singing everything from *"Good King Wenceslaus"* down to the ordinary Tommies' song, and ended up with *"Auld Lang Syne."* which we all, English, Scots, Irish, Prussians, Wurtembergers, etc., joined in. It was absolutely astounding, and if I had seen it on a cinematograph film I should have sworn that it was faked! . . .

*Sir Edward Hulse*

## CHRISTMAS 1917

Our wonderful old Corporal quickly rigged up a dear little Primus stove he had carried up, and we set it working in a funk-hole. The only old regular, a more or less freelance, crawled over from Coy H.Q. and whispered to me that at least six of the dead, just in front of us, had only just been killed half-an-hour ago: he advised us to crawl out and get their water bottles and their iron rations of tea and sugar. So, taking it in turns, we each did as suggested: this was a very useful supplement and helped us to last out until Boxing Night when we were due to be relieved - we hoped - by the Worcesters.

Apart from a few shells both ways we were having it nice and quiet and, on the night of the 24th, our Sarg crawled from Coy H.Q. with an armful ration of rum. After this, it was difficult to avoid singing, particularly as we could hear Jerry doing the same, sounding quite near. At about first light on Xmas morning, one of the bravest men I ever saw got up out of the opposite positions with a Red Cross flag. I afterwards heard him called out 'Don't shoot, Tommy, it is Christmas' and one of our stretcher bearers, having no flag, held up his arm to show his Red Cross armlet. Between them, these two unarmed men arranged to collect the personal belongings and photos of the dead to send back to relatives. Not only did both sides respect the truce, but it continued without a shot being exchanged until - hard luck - Boxing Night. It had been snowing over Xmas and we were able to melt it to further supplement our water.

With a full moon it was almost as light as day and, looking in the direction we expected our relief, I must admit I was very scared when I saw them trickling over in single file like ants in several lines. Jerry also saw them: up went his red and green flares and over came the shells on the poor Worcesters. By scattering, a good two-thirds got through and our Corporal and myself pulled them into our small

ench. By this time, our own artillery got going and
he two-way barrage produced a wonderful protective
aze, head-high.

ur Sarg came over and asked how many Worcesters
e had - we said six. 'Consider yourselves relieved,'
e said, 'get out quick, don't bunch together, muster
he other side of Waterloo dump.'

think that night was the last time I could qualify
or the Olympic Games - the Lewis Gun on my
houlder might have been a pea-shooter! Anyone
ho reached the dump before me must have had a
loody big start!

*F. Gentry*

# HUSH! HERE COMES A WHIZZ-BANG

Hush! Here comes a whizz-bang, Hush! Here comes a whizz-bang; Now, you sol-diers, get down those stairs—

Down in your dug-outs and say your pray'rs. Hush! Here comes a whizz-bang, And it's mak-ing straight for

you:— And you'll see all the wonders of No Man's Land If a whizz-bang (*bang*) hits you.—

Air "Hush! here comes the Dream Man" by permission of Messrs B. Feldman & Co.

5.—But when the General got his pudding, he was a bit puzzled. Could'nt make it out; it was so tough. "You plockhead!" he roared. "You vas boil der pudden as hard as a bomb." Then he gave the supposed pudding a vicious rap.

6.—And the General got a surprise. Yes, he won't want any more pudding this 'Xmas. "Ha, ha!" cried Cuffy, "we've done that very neatly, but we'd better grease off; it's time we were out of the picture. Besides, we want to sample the Kaiser's pudding.

## FORM PLATOON

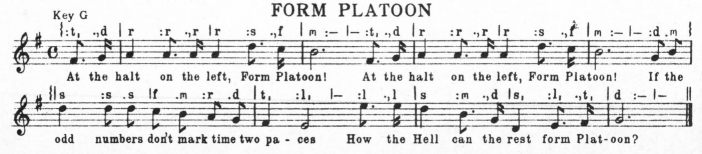

At the halt on the left, Form Platoon! At the halt on the left, Form Platoon! If the

odd numbers don't mark time two pa-ces How the Hell can the rest form Plat-oon?

## Soldier's Lullaby.

"SING me to sleep where bullets fall,
    Let me forget the world and all ;
Damp is my dug-out, cold are my feet,
Nothing but bully and biscuits to eat.
Sing me to sleep in some old shed,
A dozen rat-holes around my head,
Stretched out upon my waterproof,
Dodging the raindrops from the roof.

Far, far from Ypres I long to be,
Where German snipers can't pot at me ;
Think of me crouching where the worms creep,
Waiting for someone to sing me to sleep
                    T. SARL-WILLIAMS.

## DREAMERS

Soldiers are citizens of death's grey land,
    Drawing no dividend from time's tomorrows.
In the great hour of destiny they stand,
    Each with his feuds, and jealousies, and sorrows.
Soldiers are sworn to action; they must win
    Some flaming, fatal climax with their lives.
Soldiers are dreamers; when the guns begin
    They think of firelit homes, clean beds and wives.

I see them in foul dug-outs, gnawed by rats,
    And in the ruined trenches, lashed with rain,
Dreaming of things they did with balls and bats,
    And mocked by hopeless longing to regain
Bank-holidays, and picture shows, and spats,
    And going to the office in the train.

*Siegfried Sassoon*

## The Sentry

We'd found an old Boche dug-out, and he knew,
And gave us hell, for shell on frantic shell
Hammered on top, but never quite burst through.
Rain, guttering down in waterfalls of slime,
Kept slush waist high that, rising hour by hour,
Choked up the steps too thick with clay to climb.
What murk of air remained stank old, and sour
With fumes of whizz-bangs, and the smell of men
Who'd lived there years, and left their curse in the den,
If not their corpses . . .
                    There we herded from the blast
Of whizz-bangs, but one found our door at last.
Buffeting eyes and breath, snuffing the candles,
And thud! flump! thud! down the steep steps came thumping
And sploshing in the flood, deluging muck –
The sentry's body; then his rifle, handles
Of old Boche bombs, and mud in ruck on ruck.
We dredged him up, for killed, until he whined
'O sir, my eyes – I'm blind – I'm blind, I'm blind!'
Coaxing, I held a flame against his lids
And said if he could see the least blurred light
He was not blind; in time he'd get all right.
'I can't,' he sobbed. Eyeballs, huge-bulged like squids',
Watch my dreams still; but I forgot him there
In posting next for duty, and sending a scout
To beg a stretcher somewhere, and floundering about
To other posts under the shrieking air.

Those other wretches, how they bled and spewed,
And one who would have drowned himself for good, –
I try not to remember these things now.
Let dread hark back for one word only: how
Half-listening to that sentry's moans and jumps,
And the wild chattering of his broken teeth,
Renewed most horribly whenever crumps
Pummelled the roof and slogged the air beneath –
Through the dense din, I say, we heard him shout
'I see your lights!' But ours had long died out.

WILFRED OWEN

### KAISER'S NEW BOAST.

**" Definite End of British Spring Offensive."**

AMSTERDAM, Saturday.

An official telegram from Berlin states that the German Emperor has sent the following telegrams to the Emperor of Austria and to the German Empress :—

*To the Emperor of Austria.*

In a tenacious struggle and prepared for further battles the army on the Isonzo has bidden defiance to the mighty and stubborn onslaught of the enemy and made it fail. I congratulate thee and thy brave troops on thy great success. God will further be with us.—(Signed) Wilhelm.

*To the Empress.*

According to the report of Field-Marshal von Hindenburg, the great British and French spring offensive has come to a definite end. Prepared for since the autumn and announced since the winter, the storming English and French armies, supported by powerful masses of artillery and by technical resources of all kinds, have failed after a hard struggle of seven weeks.

God's aid has been granted to our incomparable troops and has given them superhuman force to accomplish these excellent deeds and to endure successfully in the mightiest battles ever waged in the history of war. They are all heroes. Their deeds command the respect and gratitude which every German must show them. Praise and glory be to the Lord for His help and our thanks to Him for such a magnif people in arms.—(Signed) Wilhe —Reuter.

# LORD KITCHENER DROWNE

## Admiral Jellicoe's Tragic Message from the Grand Fleet.

## CRUISER SUNK WEST OF ORKNEYS.

### Only Some Bodies and Capsized Boat Found Up To the Present—Mined or Torpedoed.

## NO SURVIVORS FROM WARSHIP.

### Tsar's Invitation to Late War Minister to Discuss Military and Financial Questions.

PRESS BUREAU, Tuesday, 1.40 p.m.

The Secretary of the Admiralty announces that the following telegram was received from the Commander-in-Chief of the Grand Fleet at 10.30 (B.S.T.) this morning :—

I have to report with deep regret that his Majesty's ship Hampshire (Captain Herbert J. Savill, R.N.), with Lord Kitchener and his Staff on board, was sunk last night about 8 p.m. to the west of the Orkneys, either by a mine or torpedo.

Four boats were seen by observers on shore to leave the ship. The wind was N.N.W., and heavy seas were running. Patrol vessels and destroyers at once proceeded to the spot, and a party was sent along the coast to search; but only some bodies and a capsized boat have been found up to the present.

**As the whole shore has been searched from the seaward, I greatly fear that there is little hope of there being any survivors. No report has yet been received from the search party on shore.**

H.M.S. Hampshire was on her way to Russia.

### SIR H. F. DONALDSON AMONG THE LOST.

The Secretary of the War Office notifies with reference to the announcement of the loss of H.M.S. Hampshire that the special party consisted of

Lord Kitchener, with

Lieutenant-Colonel O. A. Fitzgerald, C.M.G., Personal Military Secretary.

Brigadier-General W. Ellershaw.

Second-Lieutenant R. D. Macpherson, 8th Cameron Highlanders.

Mr. H. J. O'Beirne, C.V.O., C.B., of the Foreign Office.

Sir H. F. Donaldson, K.C.B., and Mr. L. S. Robertson, of the Ministry of Munitions.

Mr. L. C. Rix, shorthand clerk.

Detective Maclaughlin, of Scotland Yard, and the following personal servants :—Henry Surguy, Shields. Walter Gurney and Driver D. C. Brown, R.H.A., were also attached to the party.

### WAR CHIEF'S IMPORTANT MISSION.

Lord Kitchener, on the invitation of his Imperial Majesty, had left England on a visit to Russia. The Secretary of State was, at the request of his Majesty's Government, to have taken the opportunity of discussing important military and financial questions.

# N HIS WAY TO RUSSIA

## CAMPING OUT

We set to work on the bumps we saw in the snow, yes they were tents alright. We cleared the snow and had the tents arranged in lines when the remainder of the troops arrived, we pitched our tents and lined the wet ground with our ground sheets. Next thing was water, and the cooks were told to get it from the river close by. That was alright, it was getting dark then, but in the morning when we looked up stream and saw men washing down their horses in it, well it don't bear thinking about. The Greeks appeared very hostile and did not seem to like the idea of us being there. The only bit of humour was one morning some kids came round with single sheets of newsprint calling "Balkan News". Good news this morning, Kitchener drowned, yes it was true, he had gone down in the Hampshire. Nobody got terribly excited, all were too fed up with our conditions. The weeks dragged on, water carts were supplied and fresh water arrived daily, but even that had to be boiled. Then real trouble started, dysentery, malaria, the lot. If anybody who has suffered with this, will know what I am talking about. I had both together and was eventually picked up by some ammunition carriers and taken to the Canadian Field Hospital on one of their mules.

*from Tom Green's Journal*

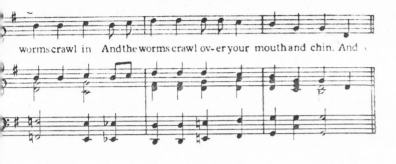

worms crawl in And the worms crawl ov-er your mouth and chin. And

as for your soul no man can tell Whether it goes to Heaven or Hell.

Do you ever think
As a hearse goes by
That it won't be long
Until you and I
Go rolling by
In a nice new shirt,
And then they lay us
Right under the dirt.

And the worms crawl out
And the worms crawl in
And the worms crawl over
Your mouth and chin.

And as for your soul
No man can tell
Whether it goes
To Heaven or Hell.

### GROUSING.

TUNE: "*Holy, Holy, Holy.*"

Grousing, Grousing, Grousing,
Always blooming well grousing.
Roll on till my time is up,
And I shall grouse no more.
Grousing, Grousing, Grousing,
Always blooming well grousing.
Roll on till my time is up,
And I shall grouse no more.

Marching, Marching, Marching,
Always ruddy well marching.
Marching all the morning,
And marching all the night.
Marching, Marching, Marching,
Always ruddy well marching.
Roll on till my time is up,
And I shall march no more.

Raining, Raining, Raining,
Always bally well raining.
Raining all the morning,
And raining all the night.
Raining, Raining, Raining,
Always bally well raining.
Roll on till my time is up,
And I shall grouse no more.

## BY DIVINE RIGHT

You must know that I feel that every step in my plan has been taken with the Divine help—and I ask daily for aid, not merely in making the plan, but in carrying it out, and this I hope I shall continue to do until the end of all things which concern me on earth.

*Sir Douglas Haig*

## OUT OF THE DEPTHS

Nasmith raised periscope shortly after noon in the centre of the harbour, and immediately there occurred one of those incongruous, incidents which pleased him. 'Our manœuvring,' he uased to say, 'was rather difficult because of the cross-tides, the mud, and the current, but most particularly on account of a damn' fool of a fisherman who kept trying to grab the top of my periscope every time I raised it to take an observation. I don't think he had any idea what it was, but to get rid of him I gave him a chance to get a good hold on it. Then I ordered "Down periscope quickly" and almost succeeded in capsizing his boat. When I looked at him a minute later he wore the most amazed and bewildered expression I ever hope to see.'

*William Guy Carr*

*When Cradock and his men went down*
 *In the far-off southern sea,*
*They thought our last Good Hope would drown,*
 *And the Huns, they yelled for glee :*
 *But " wait for a bit," said we.*
 *And we sent the strong Sturdee,*
*And he smashed those Huns with their pirate guns*
 *To the bottom of that southern sea,*
 *And the paths of trade were free !*

*When our babes on the North Sea shore*
 *Were murdered at their play,*
*When the skies dropped death on a cobbler's store*
 *At the end of a weary day :*
 *We mourned for our wee things gay,*
 *And we put their toys away ;*
*But our hearts grew strong at the sight of wrong,*
 *And we longed for the reckoning day,*
 *When there'd be Old Nick to pay !*

*When the jackal ships of Kiel*
 *Sneaked over the Northern Sea,*
*They were met by a bristling wall of steel*
 *And our stout Sir Dave Beattee,*
 *For a Lion in the path was he,*
 *And the jackals turned to flee ;*
*But the Tiger sprang, and our guns they sang,*
 *" That's one for the gay bairnie—*
 *The dear little dead bairnie ! "*

A NAVY BALLAD FOR THE NURSERY
BY J. LEWIS MILLIGAN

THE U-BOAT'S WORK IN THE MEDITERRANEAN: A TORPEDOED BRITISH TRANSPORT ABOUT TO MAKE THE FINAL PLUN

### HEARTS OF OAK (1).

Come, cheer up, my lads, 'tis to glory we steer,
To add something new to this wonderful year;
To honour we call you, not press you like slaves,
For who are so free as the sons of the waves?

BAMFORTH (COPYRIGHT).

### HEARTS OF OAK (2).

Hearts of oak are our ships,
  Jolly tars are our men;
We always are ready;
Steady, boys, steady;
  We'll fight and we'll conquer
    again and again.

BAMFORTH (COPYRIGHT).

### HEARTS OF OAK (3).

We ne'er see our foes but we wish them to stay,
They never see us but they wish us away;
If they run, why, we follow, and run them ashore,
And if they won't fight us, we cannot do more.

BAMFORTH (COPYRIGHT).

## UP AND OVER

*1st July.* On the fourth morning at 7.30, dazed by
the shelling which had begun at dawn, warm and
sleepy with rum, Horden stumbled forward blindly
across No Man's Land. It seemed to him that he was
alone in a pelting storm of machine-gun bullets, shell
fragments, and clods of earth. Alone, because the
other men were like figures on a cinematograph
screen—an old film that flickered violently—everybody
in a desperate hurry—the air full of black rain. He
could recognize some of the figures in an un-
interested way. Some of them stopped and fell
down slowly. The fact that they had been killed
did not penetrate to his intelligence. He saw with
mild surprise the figure that was Jewson disappear in
a fountain of earth. He saw with indifference the
figure that was Bennison fall down and scramble up
again. They were unreal to him. His mind was
numbed by noise, the smoke, the dust—unable to
apprehend anything but the necessity for hurrying on—
on, on—out of the storm.

When they reached the German barbed wire a measure
of lucidity returned to him. The entanglement had not
been effectively destroyed by the bombardment. He
ran hither and hither with the others to find an opening; tore madly through a partial gap, and fell into
a flattened trench. There was no one in the trench. It
had been abandoned. They must go on. On, on! They
dared not stop. The earth spouted everywhere. Hadn't
the barrage lifted?

He plunged along with bowed head as though in a
snowstorm. He realized now that men were being
killed, that his own turn might come at any moment.
He bent his head lower. If he was hit, let it not be in
his face. It would hurt to be shot in the face . . . Blast
the bloody wire! . . . He raised his head slightly.
Bennison was there on his right, a little in front. There
seemed queerly few other men. He squinted to left
and right. 'Don't bunch,' they had been told. They
weren't bunching . . . .

Another trench. Dead Germans in silly attitudes,
their faces the colour of dirty bone. Dribbles of
blood . . . No stopping. On, on, stupidly, drunkenly—
the five-mile race at school . . . A man there, stopping,
shaking his arm, flicking his hand off, softly col-
lapsing. . . . Benny gesticulating, urging him to hurry.
Bullets coming from behind now, from the left as
well, right across their path . . . Barbed wire leaping
and scratching like wild cats . . . Benny running.
Himself sprinting, panting, all his equipment
bumping on his body, belabouring him. Jump!
Into a trench. Doubled up — out of breath.

He stood up. He was alone in a firebay which was
the wrong way round. It was a deep trench, intact
at the point where he had entered it. Was it occupied?
Where was Benny? He gripped his rifle, and waited
irresolutely, sitting on the firestep. What now?
He took a bomb out of his pocket and put it
beside him. Why not stay where he was safe? No
shells were falling here, and he was sheltered from
the stream of machine-gun bullets flowing musically
overhead. 'Yes, I'll stay here,' he said aloud. Then,
instantly, 'No, you won't, you bloody little coward.
You'll go on with the others.'

He forced himself to his feet. A grey-uniformed
figure lurched round the corner of the trench. He
snatched up his bomb and flung it full in the
German's face.

'Christ. That must have hurt,' he said. 'I forgot to
pull the pin.'

The German had fallen to his knees. Horden stood
over him. Should he stick him with his bayonet, or
shoot him? The German lifted his face. The nose was
smashed and bloody. Horden saw that the man's
uniform was soaked with blood at his shoulder. He
was already wounded. He had no weapons.
'I'm awfully——' Horden began, and realized with a
rush the absurdity of the situation. About to apologise,
was he? 'Bloody fool!' he said to himself, and went

quickly out of the firebay in the opposite direction. As he turned the corner he saw the light of a signal flare and the pale star of a rocket. The trench was broken down here. Bodies stretched across his path. English and German overlapping. He tried to avoid treading on them. Impossible. He turned another corner. Shelling began again. The air was thick with dust and things that sobbed and moaned and sang and whistled. Good God! He was piddling in his trousers. A shell burst on the parapet. He jerked himself down. Loose earth rained upon him. He lay there, incapable of movement, paralysed. He had no feelings.

*Daniel George*

## HOW TO DIE

Dark clouds are smouldering into red
   While down the craters morning burns.
The dying soldier shifts his head
   To watch the glory that returns;
He lifts his fingers toward the skies
   Where holy brightness breaks in flame;
Radiance reflected in his eyes,
   And on his lips a whispered name.

You'd think, to hear some people talk,
   That lads go west with sobs and curses,
And sullen faces white as chalk,
   Hankering for wreaths and tombs and hearses.
But they've been taught the way to do it
   Like Christian soldiers; not with haste
And shuddering groans; but passing through it
   With due regard for decent taste.

*Siegfried Sassoon*

Mrs. K. Mitchley,

       C A M B R I D G E..

Dear Mrs. Mitchley,

       In reply to your letter received, I very much regret to have to inform you that your son, 34773, Pte H. J. Mitchley, was killed on the 10th of April 1918 during the severe fighting in the Battle of Armentieres.
I must apologise to you for your not having received any notification from this Battn., but our casualties have been so heavy amongst Officers, that this doubtlessly explains your not having heard anything, and I have been so inundated with letters that it has been impossible for me to give information of all the casualties concerned.
Please accept my deepest sympathy in this, your sad bereavement, and I hope that you will have some little consolation in the fact that your son died facing the enemy, and doing his duty to the last.

        Yours sincerely,

        *H. R. Thomson*

                     Lt. Col.
     Comdg. 5th Battn. Yorks. Regt.

IN THE FIELD May 14th, 1918.

# FOR YOU BUT NOT FOR ME

Key F

The bells of Hell go ting-a-ling-a-ling For you but not for me: And the

lit - tle dev - ils how they sing-a-ling-a-ling For you but not for me O

Death, where is thy sting - a-ling-a-ling, O grave, thy vic - tor - y? The

bells of Hell go ting - a-ling-a-ling For you but not for me ⎯⎯

From a sketch by a British officer.

BOMBING AN ENEMY TRENCH UNDER COVER OF NIGHT

*The Rear-Guard*

(Hindenburg Line, April 1917)

Groping along the tunnel, step by step,
He winked his prying torch with patching glare
From side to side, and sniffed the unwholesome air.

Tins, boxes, bottles, shapes too vague to know;
A mirror smashed, the mattress from a bed;
And he, exploring fifty feet below
The rosy gloom of battle overhead.

Tripping, he grabbed the wall; saw someone lie
Humped at his feet, half-hidden by a rug,
And stooped to give the sleeper's arm a tug.
'I'm looking for headquarters.' No reply.
'God blast your neck!' (For days he'd had no sleep,)
'Get up and guide me through this stinking place.'

Savage, he kicked a soft, unanswering heap,
And flashed his beam across the livid face
Terribly glaring up, whose eyes yet wore
Agony dying hard ten days before;
And fists of fingers clutched a blackening wound.

Alone he staggered on until he found
Dawn's ghost that filtered down a shafted stair
To the dazed, muttering creatures underground
Who hear the boom of shells in muffled sound.
At last, with sweat of horror in his hair,
He climbed through darkness to the twilight air,
Unloading hell behind him step by step.

SIEGFRIED SASSOON

## Trench Duty

Shaken from sleep, and numbed and scarce awake,
Out in the trench with three hours' watch to take,
I blunder through the splashing mirk; and then
Hear the gruff muttering voices of the men
Crouching in cabins candle-chinked with light.

Hark! There's the big bombardment on our right
Rumbling and bumping; and the dark's a glare
Of flickering horror in the sectors where
We raid the Boche; men waiting, stiff and chilled,
Or crawling on their bellies through the wire.
'What? Stretcher-bearers wanted? Someone killed?'
Five minutes ago I heard a sniper fire:
Why did he do it? . . . Starlight overhead –
Blank stars. I'm wide-awake; and some chap's dead.

SIEGFRIED SASSOON

# What it Really Feels Like
To be on patrol duty at night-time.

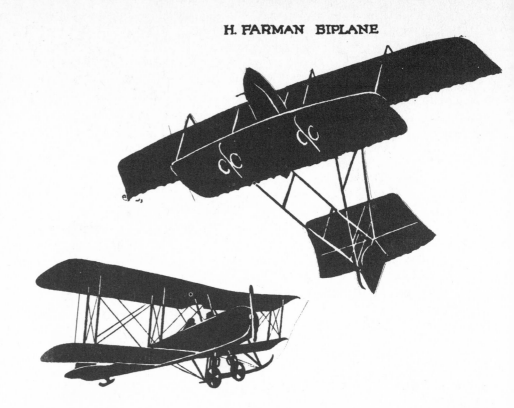

**H. FARMAN BIPLANE**

**AVRO BIPLANE**

— The Motherland — — Das Vaterland —

AWFULLY SIMPLE!          SIMPLY AWFUL!!

The reprisals of the Allied airmen have aroused great indignation in Germany, where their feat is treated as "a senseless procedure" and "a foul attack."

## 73. ODE TO THE R.A.F. (Engine).

Variation No 1

Variation No 2

Eight little cylinders sitting facing heaven,
One blew its head off—then there were seven.
Seven little cylinders used to playing tricks,
One warped its inlet valve—then there were six.
Six little cylinders working all alive,
One got a sooted plug—then there were five.
Five little cylinders working all the more,
One overworked itself—then there were four.
Four little cylinders flying o'er the sea,
One shed a piston ring—then there were three.
Three little cylinders wondering what to do,
One over-oiled itself—then there were two.
Two little cylinders very nearly done,
One broke a valve stem—then there was one.
One little cylinder trying to pull round seven,
At length gave its efforts up and ascended into heaven.

## Nursery Rhymes

Tune : "Hush-a-bye Baby."

Hush-a-bye, 2E, up in the blue,
Watched all the time by Archibald's crew,
When the shells burst the 2E will fall,
Down comes observer, pilot and all.

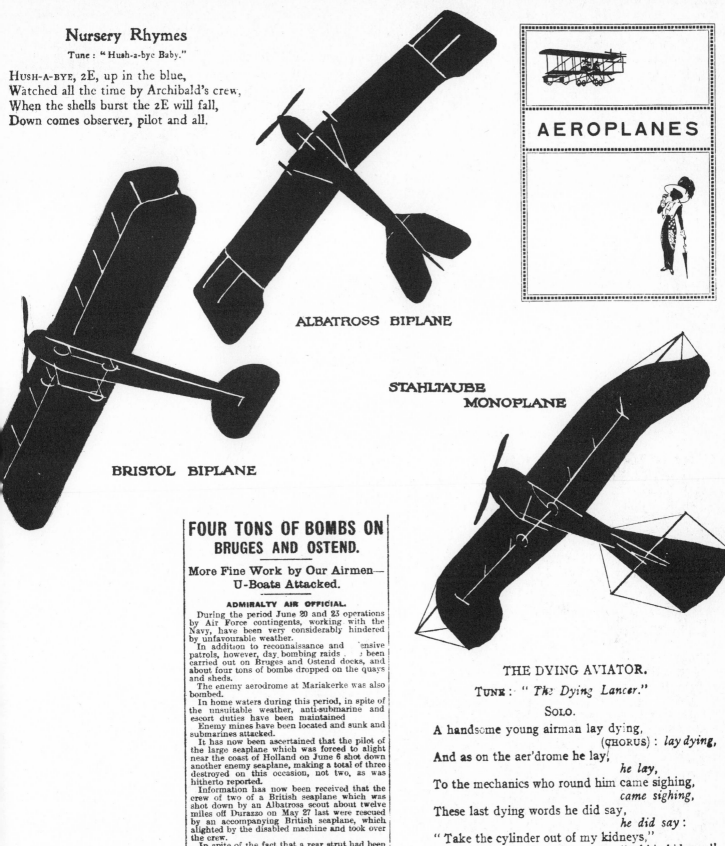

AEROPLANES

ALBATROSS BIPLANE

STAHLTAUBE MONOPLANE

BRISTOL BIPLANE

## FOUR TONS OF BOMBS ON BRUGES AND OSTEND.

### More Fine Work by Our Airmen— U-Boats Attacked.

#### ADMIRALTY AIR OFFICIAL.

During the period June 20 and 23 operations by Air Force contingents, working with the Navy, have been very considerably hindered by unfavourable weather.

In addition to reconnaissance and offensive patrols, however, day bombing raids have been carried out on Bruges and Ostend docks, and about four tons of bombs dropped on the quays and sheds.

The enemy aerodrome at Mariakerke was also bombed.

In home waters during this period, in spite of the unsuitable weather, anti-submarine and escort duties have been maintained

Enemy mines have been located and sunk and submarines attacked.

It has now been ascertained that the pilot of the large seaplane which was forced to alight near the coast of Holland on June 6 shot down another enemy seaplane, making a total of three destroyed on this occasion, not two, as was hitherto reported.

Information has now been received that the crew of two of a British seaplane which was shot down by an Albatross scout about twelve miles off Durazzo on May 27 last were rescued by an accompanying British seaplane, which alighted by the disabled machine and took over the crew.

In spite of the fact that a rear strut had been shot away, the petrol tank shot through, and floats pierced in many places by machine-gun bullets the pilot successfully returned

## THE DYING AVIATOR.

Tune : "The Dying Lancer."

Solo.

A handsome young airman lay dying,
    (Chorus) : *lay dying*,
And as on the aer'drome he lay,
    *he lay*,
To the mechanics who round him came sighing,
    *came sighing*,
These last dying words he did say,
    *he did say:*
" Take the cylinder out of my kidneys,"
    " *of his kidneys*,"
" The connecting rod out of my brain,"
    " *of his brain*,"
" The cam box from under my backbone,"
    " *his backbone*,"
" And assemble the engine again,"
    " *again*."
" When the court of enquiry assembles,"
    " *assembles*,"
" Please tell them the reason I died"
    " *he died*"
" Was because I forgot twice iota"
    " *twice iota*"
" Was the minimum angle of glide"
    " *of glide*."

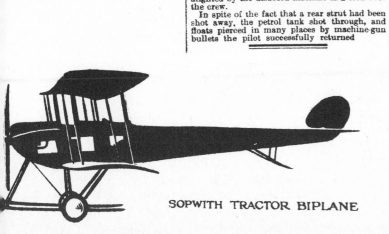

SOPWITH TRACTOR BIPLANE

## THE DAY I REMEMBER BEST

From dawn incessant artillery-fire had pounded our waterlogged sector, exploding shells hurling dis-interred fragments of assorted dead skywards, to descend, shrouded in steaming water, upon us. We were certainly earning our one-and-six-a-day pay.

Thus it was almost a relief when, in the half-light of early evening, we attacked the enemy-held forest some four hundred yards ahead.

All men experience fear; the harder part is to hide it and lead on, and as my reluctant but disciplined feet took me nearer I could see the line of heads and weapons waiting with deadly promise — but, as yet, silent!

"Why don't they fire?" "Why don't they open up?"

There was anti-climax when we found only helmeted dummies. "Jerry" had retired.

I thought my insides must be divorced from their settings, and my hair snowy-white, but had no time to dwell upon this, for within minutes I was on a 'Patrol' headed for the forest's dark depths.

Sent back to report, it was inevitable that I should fall into a deep, vile-smelling crater, complete with all mod. cons: water, mud, tangled wire, plus a very dead body.

Caught fast in the wire I fought to tear myself free, especially from the nauseating corpse almost face to face with me. Pale light from a distant flare shewed briefly the dead man, to whom I was clamped by the grasping barbs of wire ..... *Surely he was holding me to him!*

"Years" later, freed and away from that hell-hole, I delivered my message and sank down to recover — but not for long.

A hand came through the wall of darkness, and my Sergeant's voice asked whom he had the honour to meet? Sadly, I told him.

"You ain't 'arf a lucky bloke" he chuckled. "You will go and find the Irish, and guide 'em in 'ere!"

"ME, Sergeant?" I protested. "You know I'm the world's worst guide."

He admitted he knew but — I would go and find the Irish and guide 'em in 'ere, or else. 'When they're IN, we're OUT,' he promised.

The Irish found me, and I lost them, but somehow we arrived, a moment coinciding with my departure — I had no desire to listen to the Irish.

Next morning, in Camp, the "Clothing Inspection" found me with a trouser-leg flapping from waist to knee, earning much comment from the Quartermaster-Sergeant.

He finalised with 'This war is corstin' SIX MILLION QUID a day, an' you — you 'orrible man — tears yer trouser-leg orf!'

'You gotta needle an' cotton . . . SEW IT HUP!'

*A. A. Payne*

## ATTACK

At dawn the ridge emerges massed and dun
In the wild purple of the glow'ring sun,
Smouldering through spouts of drifting smoke that shroud
The menacing scarred slope; and, one by one,
Tanks creep and topple forward to the wire.
The barrage roars and lifts. Then, clumsily bowed
With bombs and guns and shovels and battle-gear,
Men jostle and climb to meet the bristling fire.
Lines of grey, muttering faces, masked with fear,
They leave their trenches, going over the top,
While time ticks blank and busy on their wrists,
And hope, with furtive eyes and grappling fists,
Flounders in mud. O Jesus, make it stop!

*Siegfried Sassoon*

## APRÈS LA GUERRE.

Après la guerre fini,
Oh, we'll go home to Blighty ;
But won't we be sorry to leave chère Germaine,
Après la guerre fini.

Après la guerre fini,
English soldier parti,
Mam'selle français beaucoup picanninies,
Après la guerre fini.

## THE WRONG WAR

We ducked in alarm as the squadron spurred their horse into a gallop and came straight at us. With a thunderous drumming of hoofs they took our trench in their stride. From the bottom, as I cowered down, I had a momentary glimpse of a horse's belly and powerful haunches as they were over and away like the wind, sword in hand.

They spread out as they went into two lines and were half-way across the open when there came a sudden pulsating blast of fire, and gaps appeared in the double line. Bullets came hissing about our heads. A man a couple of yards away from me slithered down to his knees, and then sprawled full length on the floor of the trench. Realizing our danger we ducked. Looking down I saw blood gushing from a wound in his throat. . . .

Then uncontrollable excitement possessed me and, defying the bullets, I raised my head and looked at the cavalry. Their ranks were much thinner now. Just as the foremost of them reached the trees they hesitated, turned and came racing back, lying low in the saddle.

The machine-guns barked triumphantly at their victory over mere flesh and blood. Only a handful of the once proud squadron put their blowing horses at the trench and lunged across to the shelter of the wood behind. Others trailed away on either side and in a moment were hidden from view among the friendly trees.

The whole thing from when we saw them first had only occupied a bare five minutes. We stared at each other in amazement. The fire died down. Looking over the top we saw that the ground in front, which before had been bare, was dotted here and there with shapeless mounds.

The screams of horses in agony pierced out ears with shrill intensity. As we looked animals struggled convulsively to their feet and galloped off at a tangent. Some of them swayed drunkenly and fell back, with their legs in the air. Smaller, more feeble movements showed that some of the troopers were still alive.

Single rifle-shots sounded, whether from our side or not, I didn't know, and by and by the horses were mercifully silent, but men moved at intervals—crawling behind the horses for cover, perhaps.

*Herbert Hill*

## THE REAR-GUARD
*(Hindenburg Line, April 1917)*

Groping along the tunnel, step by step,
He winked his prying torch with patching glare
From side to side, and sniffed the unwholesome air.

Tins, boxes, bottles, shapes too vague to know;
A mirror smashed, the mattress from a bed;
And he, exploring fifty feet below
The rosy gloom of battle overhead.

Tripping, he grabbed the wall; saw someone lie
Humped at his feet, half-hidden by a rug,
And stooped to give the sleeper's arm a tug.
'I'm looking for headquarters.' No reply.
'God blast your neck!' (For days he'd had no sleep.)
'Get up and guide me through this stinking place.'

Savage, he kicked a soft, unanswering heap,
And flashed his beam across the livid face
Terribly glaring up, whose eyes yet wore
Agony dying hard ten days before;
And fists of fingers clutched a blackening wound.

Alone he staggered on until he found
Dawn's ghost that filtered down a shafted stair
To the dazed, muttering creatures underground
Who hear the boom of shells in muffled sound.
At last, with sweat of horror in his hair,
He climbed through darkness to the twilight air,
Unloading hell behind him step by step.

*Siegfried Sassoon*

125

## OUT OF IT ALL

Out of the house next to which I am standing appear
three Germans. They are holding up their hands. One
has his foot in a bandage and is being helped along
by the others. They look frightened and miserable.
While they are chattering in German, a wounded
Grenadier turns up quite off his head.

'That's all right, sir,' he addresses me. 'I'll kill
them.'
'I wouldn't do that,' I remonstrate.
'Oh, that's quite all right. You just leave them to
me.' He threatens them with his rifle. The wounded
German starts to whimper and shuffles off.

The Grenadier follows, herding his little party
together. He uses his rifle like a shepherd's staff.
Could he have been a shepherd in civilian life? They
disappear in the direction of an out-house. Whatever
happened to them? They were not heading strictly
for the British lines.

Another small party of prisoners appears with a
wounded Grenadier as escort. He is dazed and shaking
with fright.
'Take a door off this house and have these prisoners
carry back this wounded man.' But he doesn't
understand.

The prisoners stand nervously about wishing to be
gone. I show them what I want done and they comply
with alacrity. Soon they are off, carrying the wounded
Grenadier. It must be a heavy load. I could not help
fearing they would drop him half-way in their eagerness
to get out of danger. But if they had any thought of
doing so it was intercepted by a German shell which
burst in their midst after they had gone two hundred
yards.

*Carroll Carstairs*

## HANS UP

*12th December.* The man who had sunk in up to his
armpits had to be handed over as trench stores.
Sgt. Dawson . . . went out into No Man's Land as
soon as the relief was completed to have a look at
the wire. He got some way into No Man's Land when
became hopelessly bogged and unable to move. He
was found by a party of five Boches who proceeded
to pull him out. He, of course, expected to be taken
off to the Hun lines, but not a bit of it. They in-
formed him that they were his prisoners and
demanded to be taken across to our trenches.
Sgt. Dawson had hopelessly lost his way and said
so, but they said it was quite all right as they knew
the way, and conducted him back to our advanced
Bn. Hqs. On the way back they picked up another
of our men, also bogged, and took him along
with them . . .

*C. J. Troyte-Bullock*

" British treachery "—by the German cari
The Hun is a liar and ghoul, too.

## DOES IT MATTER?

Does it matter? – losing your legs? . . .
For people will always be kind,
And you need not show that you mind
When the others come in after hunting
To gobble their muffins and eggs.

Does it matter? – losing your sight? . . .
There's such splendid work for the blind;
And people will always be kind,
As you sit on the terrace remembering
And turning your face to the light.

Do they matter? – those dreams from the pit? . . .
You can drink and forget and be glad,
And people won't say that you're mad,
For they'll know you've fought for your country
And no one will worry a bit.

*Siegfried Sassoon*

# MOMENT OF TRUTH

Blaven heard an order pass along the trench, and the snap of bayonets being fixed. There were three minutes to go. These men, stooping over their rifles, pushing home their sharp blades, were so close to him, so intimate and familiar; a London street, a Channel steamer, any part of the whole world then known to him would have seemed strange without brown uniformed soldiers. Yet just beyond this last line of them there were none—something else, not men, not individuals, not parts of any known world—but yet figures of men, like them, but things no one could go near, fatal, ready to kill. It was impossible to think of them as creatures having friendly feeling for each other. Blaven could only think of them as creatures seeing straight in front of them, unaware of anything to left or right, aware only of launching death straight in front.

What power on earth was going to push these men up and out into that current of death? It was nearer . . . . they'd go. He cowered lower, bullets ripped the edge of the parapet . . . . hurry, hurry . . . . thousands of bullets . . . . naked, fine, sizzling . . . . touching nothing . . . . going on, where? Men moving below, men with clothes on . . . . rifles . . . . pointed sharp bayonets . . . . that gun wasn't traversing . . . . on one line, streaming on, on, obstinate. Ah, it had swept off . . . . back again . . . . one shell . . . . another nearer . . . . this time this time.

'Sevenee and eightee and——'

Blaven's hand went up to his chin . . . . his own . . . . mud on it . . . . the stubble . . . . the soft skin below. Bang! A stone buzzed down . . . . up, up a stinger richochetted . . . . wollupy, wollupy winding spirals of sound . . . . thousands flew low, straight . . . . cutting along low.

'Time!'

Lisle shouted to his men and heaved himself out of the trench. He looked immense, aloft between the parapet and the sky. Then he was gone, all the others too; the whole trench was empty.

*Patrick Miller*

## BASE DETAILS

If I were fierce, and bald, and short of breath,
    I'd live with scarlet Majors at the Base,
And speed glum heroes up the line to death.
    You'd see me with my puffy petulant face
Guzzling and gulping in the best hotel,
    Reading the Roll of Honour. 'Poor young chap',
I'd say – 'I used to know his father well :
    Yes, we've lost heavily in this last scrap.'
And when the war is done and youth stone dead,
I'd toddle safely home and die – in bed.

*Siegfried Sassoon*

*Exposure*

29 Sept 1915. Going up, the communication-trench was crammed with stretcher-bearers and laden men going both ways. Masses of British dead lay before the uncut German wire, a fantastic display of colour from kilts, headgear, and bloody wounds on bare limbs. The mute appeal of rifles upended by the dying followed the old German line all the way to 'Tower Bridge'.

We made our way to the Hohernzollern Redoubt, on the far left of the fight. Here there had been no advance at all; only a continuing underground war. As soon as one mine was exploded, the tunnellers on both sides started others. Some of the craters descended funnel-like at least 30 feet. Almost before the last huge lumps of earth came down the storming-party would rush forward, and a desparate bombing-exchange begin. Both sides had snipers and machine-gunners doing execution from the flanks.

Our gun-position on the edge of the crater-area had little cover, and was overlooked by Fosse 8, a hotbed of snipers. 'Minnies' came over in a high graceful curve; one had seconds in which to judge where the devastating blast would come. The first night was one long alarm and stand-to.

30 Sept. We moved in at dusk for a twelve-hour shift on the lip of the crater. There was barely room for the team, and at the bottom was a pile of corpses. Shortly after dark the distress-flares went up. We must have caught the attackers: presently there was an all-clear flare and rather less din.

1 Oct. It was good to get back from the crater, even into the 'Minnie' area. Twelve hours in the crater was the limit, and we had several spells to come.

13 Oct. The battle was petering out, and 'Tower Bridge' had toppled at last.

18 Oct. Relieved, we trudged all the way back to Verquin, near Bethune.

26 Oct. Back to the Redoubt for another turn of 12 days.

*G. A. Coppard*

Our brains ache, in the merciless iced east winds that knive us . . .
Wearied we keep awake because the night is silent . . .
Low, drooping flares confuse our memories of the salient . . .
Worried by silence, sentries whisper, curious, nervous,
   But nothing happens.

Watching, we hear the mad gusts tugging on the wire,
Like twitching agonies of men among its brambles.
Northward, incessantly, the flickering gunnery rumbles,
Far off, like a dull rumour of some other war.
   What are we doing here?

The poignant misery of dawn begins to grow . . .
We only know war lasts, rain soaks, and clouds sag stormy.
Dawn massing in the east her melancholy army
Attacks once more in ranks on shivering ranks of grey,
   But nothing happens.

Sudden successive flights of bullets streak the silence.
Less deadly than the air that shudders black with snow,
With sidelong flowing flakes that flock, pause, and renew,
We watch them wandering up and down the wind's nonchalance,
   But nothing happens.

Pale flakes with fingering stealth come feeling for our faces –
We cringe in holes, back on forgotten dreams, and stare, snow-
      dazed,
Deep into grassier ditches. So we drowse, sun-dozed,
Littered with blossoms trickling where the blackbird fusses.
   Is it that we are dying?

Slowly our ghosts drag home: glimpsing the sunk fires, glozed
With crusted dark-red jewels; crickets jingle there;
For hours the innocent mice rejoice: The house is theirs;
Shutters and doors, all closed: on us the doors are closed, –
   We turn back to our dying.

Since we believe not otherwise can kind fires burn;
Nor ever suns smile true on child, or field, or fruit.
For God's invincible spring our love is made afraid;
Therefore, not loath, we lie out here; therefore were born,
   For love of God seems dying.

Tonight, His frost will fasten on this mud and us,
Shrivelling many hands, puckering foreheads crisp.
The burying party, picks and shovels in the shaking grasp,
Pause over half-known faces. All their eyes are ice,
   But nothing happens.

WILFRED OWEN

## THE COLD WAR

*Jany.* Our rations came to Bull's Trench in bags of ten, per mules, and were carried thence by human mules. No water was brought, but the ice in the shell-holes was melted to obtain water . . . . An axe would soon be the means of filling the dixies with lumps of ice. We used it for tea several days until one chap noticed a pair of boots sticking out . . . . and discovered they were attached to a body . . . .

Many people here say it is the coldest winter they have ever experienced. I filled my water-bottle at Mametz at midday with boiling hot tea, and when I reached Bull's Trench at 5 p.m. it was frozen so hard that an ordinary knife made hardly any impression on it, and we broke it instead. Each man was supplied with two pairs of gloves—one worsted pair, and "trench" gloves lined with wool . . . . We generally managed to sleep warm by sleeping close together and sharing blankets—each man carried two. The cold, however, was far prefereable to the mud.. We could move about.

*E. W. Simon*

## PUNISHMENT

In 1915 I was a gunner in the R.F.A. located in France. While serving, I was tried and punished for striking an officer, and was sentenced to ten days Number One punishment. This included being tied to a gunwheel for one hour at sundown. In the next camp to ours was an Australian brigade who had to pass through our camp in the evening to get to a nearby French town. On the first day of my sentence, they noticed me tied to the wheel. They crowded round me and asked the guard what was going on. After being told, one of them stepped forward quickly and cut me loose. This called a conference between the officers of both units, and to avoid any further trouble, it was decided that this part of my sentence should be postponed for the time being.

*G. E. Steele*

THE STAR CO'S **6**ᴰ EDITIONS
Reg. No. 287834.

APPLICATION FOR THEATRE AND MUSIC HALL SINGING RIGHTS OF THIS SONG SHOULD BE MADE TO THE PUBLISHERS.
ALL OTHER PERFORMING RIGHTS ARE CONTROLLED BY THE PERFORMING RIGHTS SOCIETY, LTD.

# TAKE ME BACK TO DEAR OLD BLIGHTY.

Written and Composed by

## A. J. MILLS, FRED GODFREY AND BENNETT SCOTT.

Sung by.

## MISS ELLA RETFORD

*Copyright.*

PRICE **6**ᵈ· NETT.
NO DISCOUNT ALLOWED.

THE STAR MUSIC PUBLISHING CO., LTD.,
51, High Street,
New Oxford Street, London, W.C.

& B. FELDMAN & CO.,
2, 3 & 4, Arthur Street,
New Oxford Street, London, W.C.

TELEPHONE: GERRARD 8446.    TELEGRAPHIC ADDRESS, "SONGONIA WESTCENT."

THIS COPY MUST NOT BE EXPORTED TO AUSTRALASIA.

Sole Australasian Agents: Dinsdale's Pty. Ltd., 269, Swanston Street, Melbourne.
Copyright MCMXVI. in England and America by the Star Music Publishing Co., Ltd.
PRINTED IN ENGLAND.

# TAKE ME BACK TO DEAR OLD BLIGHTY

A. J. MILLS, FRED GODFREY
& BENNETT SCOTT

Written and Composed by

1. Jack Dunn— son of a gun  ov-er in France to-day,____
2. Bill Spry— start-ed to fly— up in an ae-ro-plane,__
3. Jock Lee— hav-ing his tea  says to his pal Mac Fayne,__
4. One day— Mick-y O'Shea— stood in a trench some-where,__

Keeps fit— do-ing his bit— up to his eyes in clay.____
In France— tak-ing a chance— wish'd he was down a-gain.__
Look, chum— ap-ple and plum! it's ap-ple and plum a-gain!__
So brave— hav-ing a shave— and try ing to part his hair;__

Each night— af-ter a fight— to pass the time a-long,____
Poor Bill— feel-ing so ill— yell'd out to Pi-lot Brown,____
Same stuff— is-n't it rough? fed up with it I am;____
Mick yells— (dodging the shells, and lumps of dy-na-mite)____

He's got a lit-tle gram-o-phone that plays this song:____
"Stea-dy a bit, yer fool! we're turn-ing up-side down!"____
Oh! for a pot of Aunt E-li-za's rasp-b'ry jam!____
Talk of the Crys-tal Pa-lace on a Fire-work night!____

**CHORUS** *2nd time f.*
*Not too fast*

Take me back to dear old Bligh-ty,____ Put me on the

train for Lon-don Town____ Take me ov-er there,____

drop me an-y-where__ Liverpool, Leeds or Birmingham well I don't care!

I should love to see my best girl,__ Cuddleing up a-gain we soon shall

be;__ Whoa! Tiddle-y id-dle-y igh - ty, hurry me home to Bligh-ty;

Bligh-ty is the place for me.__ me.__

## TAKE ME BACK TO DEAR OLD BLIGHTY (1)

Jack Dunn, son of a gun, over in France to-day,
Keeps fit, doing his bit, up to his eyes in clay;
Each night, after a fight, to pass the time along,
He's got a little gramophone that plays this song.

## TAKE ME BACK TO DEAR OLD BLIGHTY (3).

(One day, Mickey O'Shea, stood in a trench somewhere,
So brave, having a shave, and trying to part his hair;
Mick yells (dodging the shells and lumps of dynamite)
Talk of the Crystal Palace on a firework night!

## TAKE ME BACK TO DEAR OLD BLIGHTY. (2)

Take me back to dear old Blighty, put me on the train
    for London town,
Take me over there, drop me anywhere,
Birmingham, Leeds, or Manchester—well, I don't care!
I should love to see my best girl, cuddling up again we
    soon shall be;
Whoa! Tiddley-iddley-ighty, hurry me home to Blighty—
    Blighty is the place for me.

### 'Blighters'

The House is crammed: tier beyond tier they grin
And cackle at the Show, while prancing ranks
Of harlots shrill the chorus, drunk with din;
'We're sure the Kaiser loves our dear old Tanks!'

I'd like to see a Tank come down the stalls,
Lurching to rag-time tunes, or 'Home, sweet Home',
And there'd be no more jokes in Music-halls
To mock the riddled corpses round Bapaume.

SIEGFRIED SASSOON

### I WANT TO BE IN BLIGHTY.

TUNE: "*I want to be in Dixie.*"

I want to be—I want to be—
I want to be back home in Blighty,
From where the Huns are dog-gone glad to pour
Scrambled bombs on our butter store.
I want to be—I want to be—
I want to be back home in Blighty.
You can tell the Hun I'm going to
B.L.I.—I don't know how to spell it,
But yet I'm going—Oh! yes, I'm going
To dear old Blighty land.

## BLIGHTY

The following day we sailed for Blighty, and a very rough voyage at that. I remember laying on the stretcher at Southampton. A chap in the R.A.M.C. came to me and asked where I lived. I told him London. He said when the officer comes round don't tell him London, for they don't send anyone near their home, so when the officer did come he looked at my ticket and asked where I lived. I told him the first place I thought of, Bristol. Ladies were bringing round cups of tea, chocolate, etc., and at last the stretcher bearers came and I was put into the hospital train on the top bunk and after plenty of bustle and noise, off we went and do you know where I finished up? Give you three guesses — Sunderland Infirmary, ten o'clock at night. A wire was sent home for me by one of the welfare people telling my mother where I was and not to worry. After a few days I managed to write a few lines and one morning I had a letter. How excited I was, a bit of news at last, but when I read it I nearly fell through the bed. My young brother, Bob, had been wounded during the battle on the Somme and was in St. Thomas's Hospital. I said out loud "poor little cock" and only 16 years of age. People wouldn't believe it, would they, he was one of the first volunteers for Kitchener's Army.

*from Tom Green's Journal*

**LET ME RETURN TO DREAMLAND. (1)**

There is a kingdom all my own, set in a summer sea,
Founded by two fond hearts alone, filled with love's ecstasy;
There in the dreamland garden fair, under the Heaven's blue,
Happy am I while wandering there, idling the hours with you.

### 160,000 TURKS DESERT.

WASHINGTON, Wednesday, Jan. 23.
Official despatches state that 160,000 Turks in General Falkenhayn's reorganised Turkish army deserted in less than three days during the recent journey from Constantinople to Palestine. General Falkenhayn abandoned the Palestine sector and returned to Constantinople in disgust.—Exchange.

Taxi !

## THE ROSARY—HOSPITAL VERSION.

*(To* Nurse Morris, No. 2 R.C. Hospital, Rouen.)

The hours you've tended me, dear nurse,
Are as a string of pearls to me ;
I count your hours off duty with a heavy heart,
But I'm resigned—I've got to be.

Some Nurses are—and some are not.
Some Nurses can—and some cannot.
But you're one of those that are and can ;
You're an awfu' good sport—maid to man.

And when the war is over,
You'll go back to Angleterre,
You'll hear La Belle France call you—Oh! won't
    you curse,
*Mais je ne pense pas—*'Twill be me, dear nurse

*Au revoir—pas adieu !*
AU REVOIR (NOT GOOD-BYE)

# A SPARTAN HERO.

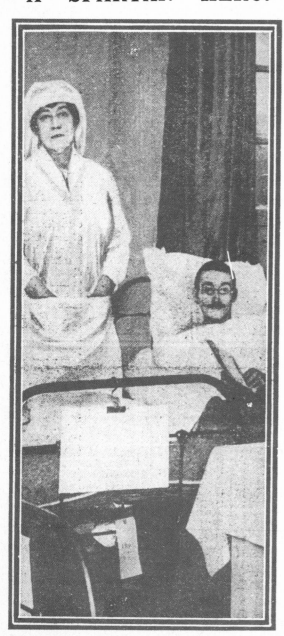

This British officer was left wounded after a battle. He
hacked off his mutilated limb with a clasp-knife, tied up
the arteries and saved his life. Such an act shows a cool
courage transcending some of the bravest deeds of war.

## ALIVE IN A SHELL HOLE FOR SEVEN WEEKS.

### ASTOUNDING ORDEAL OF A MAN WITH A BROKEN THIGH.

### HIS OWN STORY.

One of the most astounding stories of
the war is told in a supplement to the
"London Gazette" published last night.
It tells of the terrible adventure of Private J. Taylor, of the London Regiment, who lived in a shell hole which
was under fire for more than seven
weeks, with nothing to eat but bully
beef which he collected from the dead,
and nothing to drink but water which
he obtained in a waterproof cape.

Private Taylor, whose home is at Hol-
loway, receives the Distinguished Conduct Medal for "conspicuous gallantry
and devotion to duty under exceptionally
trying and terrible circumstances." The
official record of his adventure is as follows :—

"Having been cut off with his company
he received a bullet in the thigh, caus-
ing a compound fracture. To avoid capture he crawled into a shell hole, where
he remained for a period of over seven
weeks, during the whole of which time
the surrounding district was subjected
to a severe bombardment by our artillery. He subsisted on tins of bully beef
collected at night from dead bodies, and
water which he obtained in a waterproof
cape.

"After some weeks three of the enemy
visited his shell hole, but by feigning
death he avoided capture, and eventually succeeded in crawling back to our
lines—a distance of some nine hundred
yards. He displayed extraordinary
pluck and endurance by his determination not to fall into the enemy's hands."

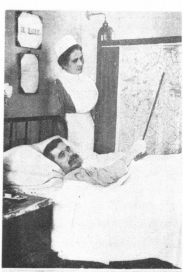

*Showing his nurse where he was wounded.*

*Fighting their battles o'er again.*

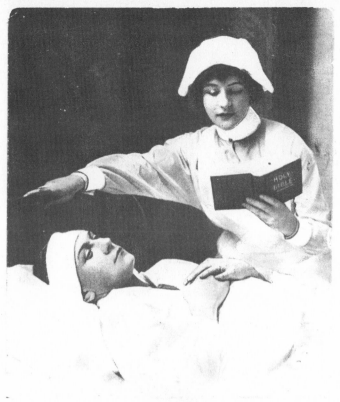

**JESU, LOVER OF MY SOUL (3).**

Plenteous grace with Thee is found,
  Grace to cleanse from every sin;
Let the healing streams abound;
  Make and keep me pure within;
Thou of Life the Fountain art;
  Freely let me take of Thee;
Spring Thou up within my heart,
  Rise to all eternity.

BAMFORTH (COPYRIGHT).

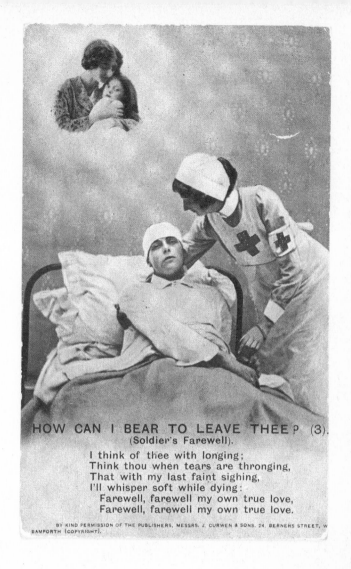

**HOW CAN I BEAR TO LEAVE THEE?  (3).**
(Soldier's Farewell).

I think of thee with longing;
Think thou when tears are thronging,
That with my last faint sighing,
I'll whisper soft while dying:
  Farewell, farewell my own true love,
  Farewell, farewell my own true love.

BY KIND PERMISSION OF THE PUBLISHERS, MESSRS. J. CURWEN & SONS. 24. BERNERS STREET, W
BAMFORTH (COPYRIGHT).

## THE EGG AND I

The War One 'Somme' offensive cost 600,000 casualties on either side and in September, 1916, I made one of that number, convinced that someone had thrown a Town Hall at me.

Finally arriving at a Birmingham Military Hospital complete with three-day-old matted bandages exposing just one eye and a corner of my mouth I was inevitably asked if I had been hit in the head! Life was like that.

Each walking-case drew personal kit, including a tin egg-cup, to be presented each breakfast-time, or else!

Twice taken to task as 'idle' I did the route-march from the ground floor messroom to the top floor Ward, returning with my egg-cup—but receiving no egg.

My egg-cup NEVER held an egg! I at no time even saw an egg! I do not believe any Walking-Wounded ever HAD an egg!

It is perhaps remarkable that in 1916 I twice forgot that egg-cup .... but for fifty two years have clearly remembered it.

Something must 'egg' me on!

*A. A. Payne*

## *In Memoriam*

Private D. Sutherland killed in action in the German
trench, May 16th, 1916, and the others who died.

So you were David's father,
And he was your only son,
And the new-cut peats are rotting
And the work is left undone,
Because of an old man weeping,
Just an old man in pain,
For David, his son David,
That will not come again.

Oh, the letters he wrote you,
And I can see them still,
Not a word of the fighting
But just the sheep on the hill
And how you should get the crops in
Ere the year get stormier,
And the Bosches have got his body,
And I was his officer.

You were only David's father,
But I had fifty sons
When we went up in the evening
Under the arch of the guns,
And we came back at twilight –
O God! I heard them call
To me for help and pity
That could not help at all.

Oh, never will I forget you,
My men that trusted me,
More my sons than your fathers',
For they could only see
The little helpless babies
And the young men in their pride.
They could not see you dying,
And hold you while you died.

Happy and young and gallant,
They saw their first-born go,
But not the strong limbs broken
And the beautiful men brought low,
The piteous writhing bodies,
They screamed 'Don't leave me, sir,'
For they were only your fathers
But I was your officer.

E. A. MACKINTOSH

## STRANGE COINCIDENCE

Anderson, McGinn and myself were stretched out in a shelter dug into the back of the trench, a shelter covered with corrugated sheeting, disguised with a covering of earth.

The sun was high and the warm day brought out the veritable thousands of big black-green bloated flies, busily searching for pieces of decayed human flesh unearthed by the bursting of shells.

High in the sky a jerry plane was busy spotting our positions and our ack ack guns were sending up shells which were bursting around the jerry plane, like the sudden opening of soft woollen bombs.

Just then, a shout from down the trench notified us that the mail was up - I slid out of the shelter to get the letters (please God), parcels, and Anderson called over to where I had been stretched out, remarking 'You're over-fat, Wilson, stay out;' with some apt reply, I went for the mail.

The threatening scream of a descending shell made me seek the shelter of a dug-out doorway and when, a minute later, I arrived back at our shelter, I found a shocked McGinn scrambling out of a pile of earth, wood and corrugated iron sheeting, and indicating that Anderson was still in the shelter.

I passed the word down the trench for stretcher bearers and, by now, several other men had arrived and we unearthed the moaning Anderson.

The stretcher bearers, having arrived, gave Anderson first-aid and bore him away to the reserve trenches.

I shudder, even today, when I think of that day - one of our ack ack shells had failed to burst and had crashed through the top of our shelter, severed Anderson's left foot, and buried itself, still un-exploded, into the bottom of the bed of earth on which Anderson had been lying.

Anderson didn't survive his ordeal and, two years later, having an accident which resulted in my left foot being amputated, I thanked God I hadn't to bear the filth, delay and tortuous journey that poor Anderson had to undergo.

*T. L. Wilson*

### To my Daughter Betty

In wiser days, my darling rosebud, blown
To beauty proud as was your Mother's prime.
In that desired, delayed, incredible time,
You'll ask why I abandoned you, my own,
And the dear heart that was your baby throne,
To dice with death. And oh! they'll give you rhyme
And reason: some will call the thing sublime,
And some decry it in a knowing tone.
So here, while the mad guns curse overhead,
And tired men sigh with mud for couch and floor,
Know that we fools, now with the foolish dead,
Died not for flag, nor King, nor Emperor,
But for a dream, born in a herdsman's shed,
And for the secret Scripture of the poor.

T. M. KETTLE

## PLAYING THE GAME

A letter arrived from my brother to say he was to
return to his unit in Chatham, the Royal West Kents,
and be tried there for being absent without leave.
A few says went by, when he wrote to tell me he
had got the same punishment as myself. I laid
awake that night and thought of him and wondered
if I should write to his C.O. and tell him he wasn't
quite 16 years of age and perhaps he would get his
discharge for being under age. After further con-
sideration I thought he may be charged for false
enlistment. I could not make up my mind what to do.
The last day of my punishment on the Saturday
afternoon, I pinched some free railway warrants and
a book of passes, whilst scrubbing out the Orderly
Room — there were four of us on this fatigue, but
the others did not see me. I got the rubber stamp
and stamped the warrants, a few passes, and tucked
them in my shirt and put the stamp back in the
drawer. On the Monday, I was given a job cleaning
up the camp and was able to go out at night into
Swindon.

One morning I received two letters, one from my
mother with a pound note and the other letter from
my brother Bob, which started with "Dear Tom, I
have been warned for the next draft, what do you
reckon to that?" I read his letter over and over
again and that afternoon I wrote to him, telling him
to get home somehow. I enclosed a pass and ten
shilling note and said I would be home when he
arrived. I made myself out a pass and used one of
the warrants for the first time. It worked O.K.
Swindon to Paddington. My mother was glad to
see me. I told her I had heard from Bob and he would
be home and we were both on embarkation leave and
he arrived the following evening. We had no ration
tickets, but managed alright. Bob and I discussed
the where do we go from here kind of thing. I had
got it all mapped out, we should go to Ireland and
join up in an Irish Regiment so that we should be
together.

*from Tom Green's Journal*

142

## ITCHY FINGERS

The startling news that there was an estaminet
functioning in some nearby cellars gave us a real
problem - how to procure cash or kind, a matter
right up Bernard's street.

He possessed two fingers the same length, able to
extract bootlaces without disturbing the wearer:
with the dawn, he departed unobtrusively to later
return with seven part-worn leather jerkins, an
issue much coveted by allied soldiery.

No-one could have been more surprised than he -
he said - when out in the open country there had
arisen a wind of unimaginable velocity driving this
bundle of jerkins into his arms with such force as
to temporarily stun him.

Recovering, he had made a protracted search for
possible owners - he said - but on failing had brought
the 'find' to the post to await possible claimants.
After deliberation, we unanimously agreed that it
would be a happy gesture to loan these to the French
occupants of this cold and cheerless section, on the
understanding that they be returned when we left
the area.

It warms my heart to remember even now how
gladly the loan was accepted and how embarrassed
we were when our most grateful and most gallant
allies insisted upon our acceptance of occasional
loans of their National uplift - bottled.

At this late date I find it impossible to say if that
area was at all times subject to atmospheric dis-
turbance but it was, I recall, most notable that
throughout our residence such pockets of aerial
pressures invariably deposited inter-changeable
articles into Bernard's lap, as it were; to the mutual
benefit and pleasure of us all.

*A. A. Payne*

# THE PHYSIOGNOMY OF FRITZ
## STUDIES IN THE FACES OF OUR PRISONERS

onth ago Mr. Hope stated in the House of Commons that we had taken 71,688 prisoners of war, of whom 55,397 were Germans. We have since brought our total bag of Germans alone up to well over 70,000. The Germans have captured fewer than half that number of our men.

British prisoners captured by the Germans

man prisoners captured by the French

## IN CLINK

I was escorted to Chiseldon Camp and the guard room. Next morning to the quartermaster's stores to draw kit and equipment, appeared in front of the C.O. and put back for District Court Martial. About 8 days elapsed. I had time to get myself polished up and was soon the old smart Tommy Green once again. It was the morning of the court held in one of the huts. I was marched in, a Colonel of the Northamptons was in the chair, the Adjutant read out the charge, a l long string, deserting His Majesty's Forces, deficient of kit, apprehended by the Civil Police, wearing civilian clothes in Dublin, dates, etc. 'You've heard the charge, what have you got to say?' said the Chairman. 'That's not my charge,' said I. The place was buzzing when he said in an angry voice 'What do you mean?' I explained I wasn't a deserter as I was presenting myself for enlistment and was apprehended in a Recruiting Office. I was immediately marched out while a conference was held and when I was marched back again I noticed desertion had been struck out and long absence substituted. My long statement was read out in court and the reason we went absent. I was marched back to the guardroom and there to wait the Court's findings. It came in a few days. The Battalion formed a square on the parade ground one morning and I was escorted to the centre, the C.O. on horseback read from sheets of paper to the effect I had been sentenced to 28 days cells. Five days after I was escorted to London to serve it in Wandsworth Prison. What a reception. I'll never forget it. They stripped everything, even to the water bottle cover. God knows what they were looking for. The screws were ordinary warders and the bloke in charge was a soldier. The treatment was terrible right from the start. German prisoners were treated better. My first surprise was Sunday morning, that was the day following my admission, first keys and plenty of shouting by the warders. 'Stand to your doors with your slops,' double back, razors, shave, locked in, razors collected. This was a scream. The bloke giving out the razors would start one end of the landing give out the razors and continue without a break collecting them up. I had a lot to learn such as having your face already lathered when the keys went in the door. Nobody told you anything. Had to pick it up as you went along. I got over the shave and slops O.K. and cleaned up my cell. Only two blankets to fold, no bedding only boards, breakfast was served, no better than the Mountjoy meal. Clean buttons ready for Chapel, keys again, stand to your doors with your stools, double from cell along the landing to staircase, and as I was still doubling at the top of the stairs with my stool on the way to Chapel, I felt a dig in the back and just above a whisper "Hello Tom, glad to see you, but not in here. It's a bastard". True words as spoken, but who was it? I knew, when we got into the Chapel, as I reached out for a prayer book being passed along, I had a shock— it was none other than Bob's pal Penfold, who I had given the free railway warrant to. I had no chance to speak to him. I discovered later he had a staff job cleaning the lavs and landing. I looked at my cell number on my return, it was K.2, 19.

On the Monday after parade, 9 till 12, all at the double, got back in my cell. I don't know what made me do it, but after removing my equipment and hanging my rifle up, went over to the shelf where my odds and ends cleaning material etc., were and happened to turn the slate over, every cell had a slate—never did know what they were for— and found it full of writing. Yes, it was written by Bob's pal, Penfold. He explained how he had got two years for forgery. It appears he had signed the warrant with his C.O.'s name, poor devil. I only just put a scribbled signature on mine and I'd defy any Bank Manager to decipher it. Still he was out of the war for two years.

We saw quite a lot of each other in the wood shed in the afternoon. We would share the same cross-cut saw and talk quietly from the side of our mouth. He tole me there was one screw who he was alright with and got little titbits on the quiet. I had to go to the workshop on Monday and get some work which has to be done in the cell, when not on parade, or the wood shed. I was doing Whipp Ends, these are lengths of rope which are bound at the ends with wax string. I soon got into the routine and the time went pretty quickly. I had 5 days remission for good conduct, one never had time to be bad anyway. At last the day came for my discharge, so I wrote the last few lines on the back of my slate to poor old Penfold. My escort arrived later in the days. As I left I was handed eight letters which had been written during my occupation of K.2, 19 in 28 days, no letters could be written or received, and no mattress, so God bless the military part of Wandsworth Prison. They certainly should be highly commended for their noble effort during World War 1.

*from Tom Green's Journal*

# I WANT TO GO HOME

No.1 IN F (Original)  No.2 IN G  No.3 IN A♭

# KEEP THE HOME-FIRES BURNING

## TILL THE BOYS COME HOME

### SONG

WORDS BY

## LENA GUILBERT FORD

MUSIC BY

# IVOR NOVELLO

PRICE 2/- NET.

U.S.A.
FRANCE

### ASCHERBERG, HOPWOOD & CREW, LTD.

IN WHICH ARE INCORPORATED THE CATALOGUES OF
E. ASCHERBERG & CO    JOHN BLOCKLEY    DUNCAN DAVISON & CO
HOPWOOD & CREW, LTD    HOWARD & CO    ORSBORN & TUCKWOOD.

16, MORTIMER STREET, REGENT STREET,
LONDON, W.

NEW YORK: LEO FEIST, INC.

# KEEP THE HOME FIRES BURNING
## Till the boys come Home

Words by
LENA GUILBERT FORD

Music by
IVOR NOVELLO

stir ing call for men. Let no
bade us do no less. For no

tears add to their hard-ship, As the Sol-diers pass a - long, And al-
gal - lant Son of Brit-ain To a for-eign yoke shall bend, And no

-though your heart is break-ing Make it sing this
Eng - lish - man is si - lent To the sa - cred

cheer - y song.
call of Friend.

149

CHORUS

Keep the Home fires burn-ing, While your hearts are yearn-ing, Though your lads are

far a-way They dream of Home; There's a sil-ver lin-ing

Through the dark cloud shin-ing Turn the dark cloud in-side out, Till the boys come

Home.　Home.

## TILL THE BOYS COME HOME (1).

They were summoned from the hillside, they were called in from
the glen,
And the country found them ready at the stirring call for men;
Let no tears add to their hardship, as the soldiers pass along,
And although your heart is breaking, make it sing this cheery song

BAMFORTH COPYRIGHT.            BY KIND PERMISSION OF ASCHERBERG, HOPWOOD & CREW, LTD.

## TILL THE BOYS COME HOME (2).

Keep the home-fires burning, while your hearts are yearning,
Though your lads are far away they dream of home;
There's a silver lining through the dark cloud shining:
Turn the dark cloud inside out, till the boys come home.

BAMFORTH COPYRIGHT.            BY KIND PERMISSION OF ASCHERBERG, HOPWOOD & CREW, LTD.

## TILL THE BOYS COME HOME (3).

Over seas there came a pleading, "Help a nation in distress!"
And we gave our glorious laddies: honour bade us do no less;
For no gallant son of Britain to a foreign yoke shall bend,
And no Englishman is silent to the sacred call of friend.

BAMFORTH COPYRIGHT.            BY KIND PERMISSION OF ASCHERBERG, HOPWOOD & CREW, LTD.

Is there a Londoner who has not visited the Grafton Galleries these last days? A string of people and cabs, extending far down Grafton Street, and a ceaseless surge inside the Galleries, passing before those amazing Canadian battle pictures—this has been the tale since the exhibition started, and has led to another extension of the date for closure until January 13.

The people who go to see these pictures are about as mixed as a packet of hundreds and thousands. Fur coats worth small fortunes brush against working-girls' sleeves. Red flannel, with decorations, rubs elbows with Private Atkins, in hospital blue, with a " bit of fluff " clinging to his sound arm. His Majesty the King drove up this week unexpectedly, but turned away again, dismayed by the crowd. . . . Inside there is a certain, peculiar subdued air over the tightly packed masses that drift from picture to picture, catalogue in hand. Not much conversation, and what there is in an undertone. It feels like a glorified kind of church . . . the valour of those deeds, recorded on every side; the horror and devastation of some of the scenes appear to grip the onlookers. Even the band plays *sotto voce.*

To look at the soldiers as *they* look at the pictures is in itself an education. . . . They do not look too long. . . . A mother, gazing from the wreckage of a battlefield to her youthful, stalwart son, whispers, " Did *you* see things like that, my darling? " And he, with an indrawn breath, says, " Oh, well, it varies, you know. It's not all quite so——." By a picture of one of the " tanks " a tall boy turns to the girl by his side—one of those would-be intelligent girls who believe in knowing things—and says, " I knew a chap who commanded one of those 'tanks.' He told me—— " " But *do* explain," interrupted the girl. " How does the postman get your letters right up into the trenches? " . . .

There is one type of female not yet extinguished by the war—impossible, vacuous, but delighted that certain headdresses are so becoming—and she must see the battle pictures with a bosom friend. Before a picture representing a captured German gun emplacement, with gruesome, twisted figures lying where they fell, this lady pauses, her immovable smile in full play. She looks at the picture, then at her friend—still smiling. " Horrible, isn't it? " she beams, and in the same breath adds, " Will you come to tea next Monday, dear? " MARGARET CHUTE.

## JUDAS AND THE PROFITEER

Judas descended to his lower Hell
　To meet his only friend – the profiteer –
Who, looking fat and rubicund and well,
　Regarded him, and then said with a sneer,
'Iscariot, they did you! Fool! to sell
　For silver pence the body of God's Son,
Whereas for maiming men with sword and shell
　I gain at least a golden million.'

But Judas answered: 'You deserve your gold;
It's not His body but His soul you've sold!'

*Osbert Sitwell*

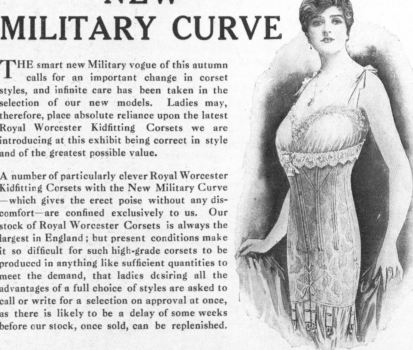

Drawn by Phyllis Spence.

**THE BANNED BUTLER**

In many houses the man butler has been replaced by a woman server.
The lady in livery is the note of the day.

---

Many mothers are informing the manufacturers that since taking MILK GRUEL twice daily, made from Robinson's "Patent" Groats, they have been able to nurse their babies.

# ROBINSON'S
## "patent" GROATS

---

## SIMPLER MEALS.

### RULES FOR HOTELS AND CLUBS.

#### MEATLESS DAYS SOON.

*Two important official announcements with regard to economy in food were issued last evening.*

*A Board of Trade Order limits meals served in hotels, clubs, and other public eating places between 6 and 9.30 p.m. to three courses, and other meals to two courses. The Order comes into force on December 18. A further Order will soon be made prohibiting, both at public eating places and at home, the eating of meat, poultry, and game on certain days.*

*Maximum prices for soldiers' meals in all licensed premises in London have been fixed, as from December 18, and such premises may be closed as a penalty for exceeding the limits authorized.*

## STATE FIXED MEALS
### IN WAR TIME.

### Dinners in Public Limited to Three Courses.

#### MEATLESS DAYS COMING.

The doom of the luxurious diner in war-time is sealed.

Twelve days from now—that is to say on and after December 18—meals in hotels, restaurants and other public places are to be limited to two or three courses.

The new regulation, which is issued by the Board of Trade as an Order under the Defence of the Realm, provides:—

**(1)** That no articles of food shall be served by or consumed in any inn, hotel, restaurant, refreshment house, boarding-house, club, mess, canteen, hall, or any other place of public eating in the form of or as part of a meal consisting of

more than three courses if the meal begins between the hours of 6 p.m. and 9.30 p.m., or of more than two courses if the meal begins at any other time.

**(2)** Plain cheese shall not be regarded as a course. Hors d'œuvre (not containing any preserved or freshly cooked fish, meat, poultry or game), dessert (consisting only of raw and dried fruit), and soup (prepared in the ordinary way which does not contain any meat, poultry or game in a solid form), shall each be computed as half a course.

---

---

## OUR DAILY WAR-TIME MENU.

### DINNER FOR THURSDAY.

Artichoke Soup.
Spaghetti Cutlets.
Prune Dessert.

#### The Recipes.

**Spaghetti Cutlets.**—Required: Six ounces spaghetti, one small onion, one dried half an ounce of margarine, a good teaspoonful of barley flour, three ounces of any kind of left over meat, a dessertspoonful of tomato sauce.

Boil the spaghetti in boiling salted water, then tender drain and chop up, add the minced meat; and season to taste. Prepare the dried egg and beat up. Heat the margarine, slice the onion finely, and cook in the fat until golden, then stir in the barley flour, to this add the spaghetti and meat, sauce, and last of all the beaten egg, stir until the mixture thickens but does not boil, and season to taste.

Put the mixture on a dish, when cold turn into cutlets, roll in fine oatmeal, and fry a golden brown on both sides in smoking fat. Garnish with parsley, and send to table with brown gravy.

**Prune Dessert.**—Required: Four ounces prunes, one gill packet of vanilla jelly crystals, a few drops of vanilla essence. Stew the prunes until tender in a little water, then take the stones out and mash to pulp. Crack the stones, take out the kernels, and chop up. Dissolve the jelly, stir into it the prune pulp and nuts, flavour with a few drops of vanilla essence, and pour into a wetted mould to set. Turn out and surround with a border of plainly boiled rice.

---

---

## The
# LORD MAYOR'S
# MESSAGE

THE retiring Lord Mayor of London, Sir Charles Hanson, has issued the following inspiring call to action :

"Four years and more have passed since first our guns flung back the insolent challenge of the War Lords.

"The Guns spoke at Jutland—and the High Seas Fleet still shuns the British Navy. They spoke in China, Africa, the Pacific ; and the German Colonial Empire is to-day little more than an evil memory.

"They spoke in Mesopotamia—and Bagdad fell ; in Palestine ; and the Last Crusade has been won. They sounded amid the crests of the Balkans ; Bulgaria heard them and surrendered.

"They echo to-day from the Adriatic to the Alps, with the promise of liberty for peoples long exiled and oppressed. They thunder to-day on the Western Front as our soldiers advance along the road that leads to final victory.

### Live to Lend

"What is the message of the guns for us, here in Britain ? They bid us redouble our effort, moral and financial. They claim from us more self-denial ; more resolution ; more of the spirit of patriotic thrift. Each one of us—each man and woman—each City and Town and Village—must be filled, in these historic hours, with a deeper sense of civic responsibility.

"We must *live to lend* our full share of the £25,000,000 required week by week. Our full share is the utmost we can possibly afford. Anything short of that would mean failure in our duty to our country and to the men behind the guns."

# FEED THE GUNS
## with
# WAR BONDS

### and help to end the War

## FALSE ALARM

I soon made myself at home and was treated with respect as my chevron on my arm was noticed, a gold and two blue, indicating active service, the gold chevron denoted abroad in 1914, the blue for each year after. I soon found myself with a draft of about 60 with an Officer in charge on our way up the line to join the main body. The regiment were holding the line at a mining town called Vermelles, not a bad sector as the front line was reached by a long tunnel which ran from the supports to the front line. The German trenches were about four hundred yards away. I remember one day I was the gas sentry, the object was to give the alarm in event of a gas attack. Of course we had been issued with real gas masks by this time which were worn on the chest. An empty shell case was usually hung on a post in the trench, and a piece of iron bar lay near and should there be an attack the sentry would immediately put on his own mask and then strike the shell and give warning. The day in question I was so intrigued with the bursting 18 pounders of ours and the Jerries diving for cover, I must have got excited seeing their transport in the road being hit, but always felt sorry for the poor horses. Suddenly I smelled a peculiar burning smell. After another sniff to make sure, I snatched my gas mask out and put it on and then belted the life out of this shell case. The cries of 'gas' came from left and right as the alarm went up all along the line. Everybody packed the trench with fixed bayonets, nobody really knew what was going on. After about an hour the cries of 'all clear' was being shouted on our right and ran all along the line. Nobody ever knew who had started the false alarm. I thought it was gas at the time, but discovered it was the smell of the cordite from the 18 pounders as they passed low over our trench. I had a little chuckle and thought it a bit of excitement anyhow.

*from Tom Green's Journal*

## WAR BABY

A long grey column marched down the Chorleywood Road. There was a British soldier in front and another behind the column, with fixed bayonets on their rifles.

'Prisoners,' said Edie, 'beastly Germans.'

'But why don't they kill the soldiers and run away?'

'Because they're cowards,' said Edie. 'They wouldn't dare attack our lads. They kill babies.'

(But they didn't kill me).

A huge lorry lurched past. Again it was in the Chorleywood Road, just where the entrance to the Masonic Girls' School now is. It had a great fat bag of gas - substitute for petrol - on its roof.

It turned over just in front of my pram.

'Brute,' said Edie, 'he might have killed us both.'

Edie's stepson, Ted, was the bravest soldier in the finest of all Regiments, which was known to us as the Beds and Hearts (twenty years later I was to serve in the same Regiment).

Ted was our hero: I wished my name were Ted.

'But your first name's Edward; you **could** be called Ted.'

I knew They wouldn't allow it. And They didn't.

Uncle Charlie was a subaltern in the Horsertilry; he wore high polished boots. I tripped over his spurs and fell howling on my face.

'Must be a little soldier what. Mustn't be a crybaby what.'

After more than half a century I still remember my hatred for Uncle Charlie.

In the freezing bathroom I was held up to the window to see a great, cigar-shaped object drifting across the night sky.

I still have a piece of that Zeppelin, pinned to a card with the statement that it was shot down at Potter's Bar, not so far away.

*Peter Tewson*

Refugee carrying a mattress in the East End.

## ALIENS HUNTED OUT OF MEAT MARKET.

### Porters' Swift Way with Germans Who Came to Smithfield.

### SHOPS LOOTED BY CROWD.

London's anger at the sinking of the Lusitania burst in a violent storm upon the heads of Germans yesterday.

German shops were pillaged by huge and riotous crowds which the police were unable to control and men known to be Germans who showed themselves in public places were very roughly handled.

The trouble began at Smithfield, where, in spite of the boycott, a number of German butchers drove up in order to obtain supplies of meat.

The meat porters in a body mobbed them and hustled them out of the market.

German butchers who venture to come to the market have to deal with three allies—the English dealers, the porters and the carriers.

"For a start," said a porter, "the dealers won't serve 'em. They've got notices up, 'No business transacted with Germans.' Then we porters wouldn't carry their pig carcases, not if they hung them with diamonds. And, last of all, the carriers wouldn't shift the meat for 'em."

#### "STRAFE HIM, BOYS."

Another German was chased across Farringdon-street into Holborn by some 300 people. He attained a marvellous speed, and the men perched on the vans and wagons shouted sporting phrases at him.

"Strafe him, boys!" shouted one stout porter, who was unable to join in the chase. The chase was long and stern, but eventually the German found sanctuary on an omnibus in Holborn, and the porters, who were by this time rein-forced by every office and errand boy within running distance, returned to the market in a body, singing "Tipperary."

Later in the morning, when the top end of the market had been drawn blank, hounds "found" in the "village." A porter announced the fact, and his colleagues at once joined in the chase. The German, realising that flight was useless, tried to explain.

"We told you yesterday the market wouldn't hold you," said a porter.

"Fair's fair," protested the German, "and I'm no friend of the Kaiser's."

"You're a German, aren't you?" said the porter in a tone which indicated that that fact sufficed.

Several policemen formed a bodyguard round the man and, with an angry crowd following, escorted him to a taxicab, in which he drove off amidst a volley of jeers.

#### UNGRATEFUL TO POLICE.

Several Germans as soon as they realised that the market was too warm to hold them rushed to their carts and drove off at breakneck speed towards Aldgate, pursued by porters, who, however, were unable to catch them.

In Aldgate the fugitives tried to obtain meat at various stalls. The public, however, lost their temper, and violently attacked the men, unhitching the horses from the carts, cutting the traces and removing the bridle and the harness.

The Germans were severely treated, and their clothes in some instances were torn from their backs, and they were battered about the head and body.

When the police, against heavy odds, tried to intervene the ungrateful enemy showed his appreciation by shouting: "To hell with England." This infuriated the mob, who chased the Germans up as far as the Minories.

Here they attacked a German butcher's shop and, going inside, hauled out the occupants.

The shop was ransacked from top to bottom, and all kinds of food flung into the street.

The English butchers and slaughterers, now reinforced, proceeded to a German barber's shop a few doors from Aldgate Station and gave him a thrashing.

The shop of an Austrian barber in High-street, Aldgate, was next attacked, the mob setting about the manager, whom they siezed and flung him into the road.

The mob looted the shop, taking possession of razors, shaving-pots, cigarettes and cigars, and practical jokers among the crowd commenced free shaving operations.

## ALIENS TO GO.

### ENEMIES OF WAR AGE TO BE INTERNED.

### PREMIER'S SPEECH.

### WOMEN TO BE SENT BACK TO GERMANY.

## Are you lathering Patriotically?

That is to say: Are you using a *British made* Shaving Stick for your morning shave?

GERMAN RESERVISTS ARRESTED AT FOLKESTONE WHEN ABOUT TO EMBARK FOR FLUSHING.

**ZEPPELIN**

## When these Ruddy Zepps are Over

Tune : "What a Friend we have in Jesus."

When these ruddy Zepps are over,
Watch us get up from our bed,
Show a ruddy ducking leg there,
But close your ears to what is said.
No more ruddy rural rambles,
No more walks with Liz and Kate,
No more ducky doodle cuddlings,
Blame the Boches' Hymn of Hate.

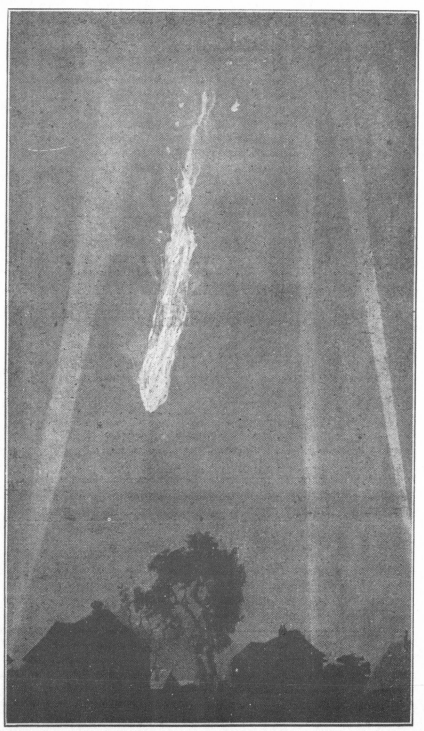

### BRIC-A-BRAC 1917

The Optimist:

I think we've done them Zeppelins brown.

The Pessimist:

They're jolly hard things to whack.

O.  Well, anyway, we've brought them down.

P.  And let lots more get back.

O.  You'll be alright and so shall I, in our little wooden hut.

P.  And we'll both come out extra dry when all the pubs are shut!

O & P  The Optimist and The Pessimist are there when the Airmen shoot.

O.  My heart beats high when the Zeppelins come.

P.  And mine is in my boots.

O.  They'll soon throw up the sponge, you'll find, we've got them on the hop.

P.  It aint what they throw up I mind - its more what they drop!

### 8,000 FEET FALL.

#### Graphic Story of German Gasbag's Dying Moments.

##### RED LIGHT—AND CHEERS.

A member of *The Daily Mirror* staff who had been called out on duty as a special constable somewhere on the eastern outskirts of London and was an eye-witness of the raid events which developed into the destruction of one of the raiding super-Zeppelins, described them thus:—
"It was at about 11.30 p.m. that I heard the first Zeppelin.
"I could not, however, see any Zeppelin owing to the mist intervening.
**Aeroplanes Cruise Round.**—"Several aeroplanes continued to cruise around at great heights with only their little tail lights, looking like travelling stars, discernible.
"People were beginning to return to bed in the assumption that the raid was over, when soon after two o'clock bombs were heard dropping again—this time in the direction of London—together with the noise of heavy anti-aircraft bombardment.

## OFFICERS AND THEM

We had been relieved and where I say marching
but really staggering to a camp of Nisson Huts a
few miles from the front line and passing through
a village named 'Vaux'. It was just a heap of bricks
and rubble. I noticed there was plenty of wood
amongst the ruins and when we reached the camp,
removed our muddy coats, putties, etc. had breakfast, few biscuits and tons of jam, I suggested a
number of us go back to this vaillage of 'Vaux' and
get some wood, make a fire and dry our clothes—we
were soaked to the skin. After much chat I managed
to get three of our hut to come with me, managed
to find some ropes and off we went, footsore as we
were, to trudge the couple of miles back to the
village. We each had a load tied up and dragged it
along the road in single file. We were laughing,
swearing and nearly exhausted when we were at
last in sight of the camp, myself leading the party,
when clippity clop and a Major on horse back
halted in front of me. Hello I thought, another
of those bastards like the one in Salonika. For king
and country I dropped my rope and saluted. 'Where
the hell do you think you're going, where did you
get that from?' I explained we had just come from
the line and was wet through and going to make
a fire. All he said was 'Take that back where you
found it'. If there was ever a provocation for
murder, none was ever greater. We turned about and
he followed us on his horse. That poor horse had
never walked so slow in its life I bet. When we did
at last reach the village, he stood and waited till
we had untied our ropes and left the wood in a heap
and made sure we were on our way empty handed.
His ears must have burned for the duration. I can
imagine him with his medals, in evening dress at
a big dinner, and writing his memoirs of the Great
War, and selling at about thirty bob a time. If
he's still alive let him get a load of this from one
of the million who were dropped by the wayside.

*from Tom Green's Journal*

## ANOTHER OUTBURST
### BY THE KAISER.

"Envious Enemies" Blamed
for the War.

## "NO GERMAN HATRED."

The Kaiser has made another attempt
to fasten the responsibility for the war on
the Allies.

In a speech to the workers at Krupp's he
declared that Germany's enemies began the
war because they envied her progress and
prosperity, and that Germany is only fighting for her existence.

Visé Paris N° 2⌐0615 ;
*YPRES. — La Rue du Verger avant et après le Bombardement.*
*Orchard street before the Bombardment and after.*

## HOLLOW SHELL

And there was the long narrow ribbon of street
utterly silent, and the walls, with nothing but ruin
behind them, aslant and tottering, till it seemed a
push with your hand would overset them: and indeed
they do collapse frequently, for we saw many heaps
of bricks, and there are large notices everywhere
warning you to walk close into the walls and not in
the middle of the streets. You can't concieve the
effect of a really big town in that state, however you
try; it is far worse than seeing the place totally
ruined, and in heaps of bricks and nothing more.
It is those ghastly, sightless, purposeless walls
that catch you, and the silence. For the life of me
I could not have talked loud; I think the echo
would have sent me mad.

*J. E. Crombie*

THERE are other children in London, the
holidays, children of the slums and the d
roads of struggling poverty. It is holiday-ti

for them, too : long hours to be spent playi
in the road or the park. No luncheon-part
come their way. . . . just bread and scra
and an old rag doll, for " make-believe
with some teeming street market and its reeki
stalls as a pleasure-ground, and a bar
organ for an orchestra.

## BACK TO FRONT

At last we managed to reach camp and leave the two miles of blue air behind. We managed to get enough fuel to dry our clothes and within a couple of days we were O.K. It was rumoured we were out for 14 days, which was good and everybody happy, until about the sixth evening, orderly sergeants were summoned to the C.O.'s hut. Orders to get dressed and everybody ready in half an hour. It appeared Jerry had broken through. We all got ready with our equipment on and sat in the hut. It was pouring with rain and the air was full of grousing and moans. No rest for the wicked someone said. Suddenly the order 'fall in' and a stream of old buses appeared. We were told off so many to each bus. The one eventually pulled up in front of my batch, to cheer me up no end I laughed outright, and I can see it now, the driver in a civi cap and pipe but the bus, not a bit of glass but a long board with the words written in bold letters 'I have no pane dear mother now'. I wonder if Bairnsfather mentioned this. We heard the gun fire long before we reached our destination with all the sky lit up. It was like Crystal Palace on a firework night. We eventually reached journey's end and I always say a bad ride is better than a good walk, so after another peep at the wording on the bus and another giggle, we were put in support, that means entrenched behind the front line ready to advance if needed, but more troops began to arrive and go right past us, still I expect they knew what they were up to. Although we couldn't fire we had a lot of killed and wounded, as we copped most of the shell fire and was glad when told to advance. We got to what we supposed to be the front line but there were no trenches. We just laid in the mud and opened fire. Every shot I fired I thought of that bloke on his horse—seemed to haunt me somehow. After hours it seemed the firing like the rain got steadier and at last just a machine gun burst here and ther. We lay soaked for a long time, then a message was passed to make our way back to the sunken road, a few at a time from the right. We assembled on the road, but alas no buses this time. We fell in and marched back drearily to the camp again. Oh, for that bloke's 'orse, I was dead tired. There were four missing from our hut, they've got tied up with the wrong mob, someone suggested, but no luck we never saw them again. Likewise many more from that night's work.

*from Tom Green's Journal*

Francis, Day & Hunter
REGᴰ Nº 257,748.
Sixpence Nett

Nº 1452 SIXPENNY POPULAR EDITION. (NO DISCOUNT ALLOWED)

# The Laddies Who Fought and Won.

## Written, Composed and Sung by

# HARRY LAUDER.

COPYRIGHT.

LONDON:
FRANCIS, DAY & HUNTER,
138-140, CHARING CROSS ROAD, W.C.
NEW YORK;
T. B. HARMS & FRANCIS, DAY & HUNTER, INC., 62-64, WEST 45ᵀᴴ STREET.

Copyright MCMXVI, by Francis, Day & Hunter.

# The Laddies who fought and won.

Written, Composed and Sung by HARRY LAUDER.

*Copyright MCMXVI, by Francis, Day & Hunter.*

F. & D. 14343.

2

*TILL READY.*

*mf*

1. There's a
2. We can

*p*

dear old la_dy, Mo_ther Brit_ain is her name, And she's
all look back to the his_t'ry of the past That has

all the world to me._____ She's a dear old
made us what we are._____ We have pledg'd our

soul, al_ways the same, With a heart as
word we all shall hold fast, Be the day a _

F. & D. 14343.

F.& D.14343.

CHORUS. *2nd time* f

When the fight-ing is over, and the war is won, And the

flags are wav-ing free, _____ When the bells are

ring-ing, And the boys are sing-ing Songs in ev'-ry

key, _____ When we all gath-er round the

old fire - side, And the old mo_ther kiss _ es her

son, _____ A' the lass_ies will be

lov_ing all the lad_dies, The lad_dies who fought and

won. _____ When the won. _____

F.& D.14343.

Printed by HENDERSON & SPALDING, Ltd., Sylvan Grove, Old Kent Road, London, S.E.

# REAT BRITISH VICTORY ON A 30-MILE FRONT.

## 0,000 PRISONERS: 200 GUNS.

### HREE ARMIES DEAL THE HUN A SMASHING BLOW.

# GERMANS FALLING BACK BEFORE BLOW.

### British Advancing—4½ Miles from St. Quentin—Attilly, Vermand and Vendelles Captured—Close to La Bassee.

AMERICAN ARMY, France, Thursday.

An attack was launched between five and eight o'clock this morning on either side of the **salient of St. Mihiel** by **Franco-American forces,** preceded by a barrage lasting four hours.

The southern attack is on a front of twelve miles and the western attack on a front of eight miles.

## THE END AT LAST.

THE armistice was inevitable after the last of the War Lords left. It is signed. The old Germany is unequivocally defeated. The biggest war in history is over. Yesterday all London heard the maroons for the last time (we hope), and this time with a cry of rejoicing. . . .

Before everything, in this hour of victory, our duty is to remember those to whom we owe it that the end has been reached so much more swiftly than any of us dared to hope a few short months ago.

We must salute, with reverence and gratitude, the memory of the ever-living dead—of that great company of brave and unselfish ones, humble or great, who in hundreds, in thousands, in millions, have died to save the world—have given their lives that we might "have life and have it more abundantly."

We must salute the wounded and suffering—the blinded, the maimed, and those whose days must pass in weakness, because they gave their strength for us.

We must salute also the great general, Marshal Foch, to whom, more than to any living man, we owe it that to-day—instead of to-morrow, instead of months and years hence—the nightmare is lifted from our minds.

It is to all these that our thoughts go to-day—toilers and sufferers, statesmen and soldiers and sailors. They have had the almost intolerable burden. Those of them who can see and hear us must have the gratitude they deserve. The others are beyond our praise.

If the news of the armistice be received with those first and saving thoughts we shall start upon the labour of Peace with a sense of the responsibility resting upon us who survive.

We shall then not disgrace our peace with thoughts and things unworthy of the sacrifice made for us. We shall be glad, but we shall be grave in our gladness. A new chapter of the world's history is beginning. It is for us to write it and we can write only the thoughts we have within us, draw only the figure and image of ourselves. That form and figure can be noble or base. It is the new choice before the world. . . .

For the rest, it is enough for the moment to note that the armistice terms do indeed register our victory. They constitute no compromise. The fact of defeat is written in plain letters before the new rulers of Germany. They cannot pretend to be deceived and they cannot deceive their people. The way for the new Germany is through recognition of the utter bankruptcy of the Prussian Germany they served.

The way for us is to be moderate in triumph and to remember what difficulties still lie before us in passing from war to peace and in securing a peace that will not lead to further wars for generations unborn.

By our thoughts and actions we shall be responsible, during the next few months, for the future of the world for centuries—a tremendous duty. Our dead have placed their achievement in our hands, for us to use or misuse. We shall be saved from all misuse of it if our first and last thoughts are constantly and only of them. W. M.

# FOCH'S DRASTIC TERMS

## Evacuation of Belgium, Alsace - Lorraine, Luxemburg and Rhine Lands.

## DURATION OF ARMISTICE, 36 DAYS.

## All U-Boats To Be Surrendered and 74 Warships Disarmed—Heligoland a Base?

The Prime Minister, in the House of Commons yesterday, gave the terms of the Armistice. The main points are as follows:—

**Immediate evacuation of Belgium, Alsace - Lorraine and Luxemburg.**

**Evacuation by enemy of Rhine lands completed within 16 days.**

### AT LAST !

#### By W. R. TITTERTON

The long day's work is done,
  The gun's last thunder dies,
The dreadful wager's won. . . .
  And yet with quiet eyes
We watch that billow of British flag
  Fill our exultant skies.

Clash out, O jubilant bells!
  Wildly as beats my heart!
White hands flutter, the loud cheer swells,
  And yet, in house and mart,
Our mothers weep for happiness;
  Our widows pray apart.

We may not stint our mirth,
  Plucked from the jaws of hell!
We breathe the freedom of the earth,
  And yet our hearts know well
The price we paid for that glad news
  Our loud-mouthed bugles tell.

We may not call them back—
  Loud as the bugles play,
Where wooden crosses mark the track
  Of our heroic clay.
And yet in endless silent line
  They hedge our streets to-day.

And yet down every street
  Their endless columns tread,
Their drums in throbbing silence beat,
  Their viewless banners spread,
Their muted bugles sound a charge
  Over the marching dead.

Bright shine our eyes; our lips
  Part in a wild hurray;
Hands meet in passionate grips;
  In thankfulness we pray
Because the stone which crushed our hearts
  The Lord hath rolled away.

### *At Last, at Last!*

\*

*Après la guerre fini*
*Tous les soldats partis,*
*Mademoiselle avec piccaninni,*
*Souvenir des Anglais.*

Railways of Alsace-Lorraine to be handed over.

Immediate repatriation, without repatriation of Germans, of Allied and United States prisoners.

All German troops in Russia, Rumania and elsewhere to be withdrawn.

Complete abandonment of the treaties of Bukarest and Brest-Litovsk.

Immediate cessation of all hostilities at sea.

To be disarmed : **6 battle cruisers, 10 battleships, 8 light cruisers, 50 destroyers** and other services.

Allies reserve right to occupy Heligoland, to enable them to enforce the terms of the Armistice.

Handing over to Allies and United States of all submarines.

Duration of the Armistice is to be **36 days**.

The Prime Minister said the terms included the surrender of ,000 locomotives, 2,500 heavy, 2,500 field and 30,000 machine guns.

# "LAST SHOT OF WAR FIRED AT 11 A.M."

## 4 YEARS 328 DAYS OF WAR.

**1914.**
Aug. 1.—Germany declares war on Russia.
Aug 3.—Germany declares war on France.
Aug. 4.—Great Britain declares war on Germany.

**1915.**
May 23.—Italy declares war on Austria.

**1917.**
March 12.—Russian revolution.
April 5.—America declares war on Germany.

**1918.**
March 2.—Russo-German peace at Brest.
Sept. 30.—Bulgaria surrenders.
Oct. 31.—Turkey surrenders.
Nov. 3.—Austria signs armistice.
Nov. 9.—Kaiser abdicates.
Nov. 11.—Germany signs armistice and hostilities cease.

**1919.**
June 28.—Peace signed with Germany.

## 30,000,000 CASUALTIES.

Appended are approximate figures of the belligerents' casualties:—

| | | | |
|---|---|---|---|
| Great Britain | 3,049,991 | Serbia | 300,000 |
| Germany | 6,385,000 | Belgium | 350,000 |
| France | 4,000,000 | Turkey | 750,000 |
| Russia | 9,150,000 | Rumania | 200,000 |
| Austria | 4,000,000 | Bulgaria | 200,000 |
| Italy | 1,407,000 | | |
| America | 236,117 | | 30,028,108 |

### 52,000,000 IN ARMS.

Below was the approximate fighting strength of the Armies engaged in the world war :—

**ALLIES.**

| | | | |
|---|---|---|---|
| Great Britain | 8,000,000 | Portugal | 120,000 |
| France | 6,500,000 | Belgium | 500,000 |
| Italy | 3,500,000 | Rumania | 500,000 |
| America | 2,000,000 | Greece | 300,000 |
| Russia | 10,000,000 | Serbia | 500,000 |
| Japan | 1,400,000 | Montenegro | 50,000 |
| Total | | | 33,870,000 |

**FOES.**

| | | | |
|---|---|---|---|
| Germany | 12,000,000 | Turkey | 1,000,000 |
| Austria-Hungary | 6,000,000 | Bulgaria | 320,000 |
| Total | | | 19,320,000 |

## WHEN THIS RUDDY WAR IS OVER.

The following is the particular version sung in the R.F.C. All these marching songs differ slightly, according to the Unit singing, a little local colour being invariably added.

When this ruddy war is over,
O ! how happy I shall be !
When this ruddy war is over
And we come back from Germany.
No more blooming kit inspection,
No more church parade for me.
When this ruddy war is over,
You can have your R.F.C.

When this ruddy war is over,
Oh ! how happy we shall be !
When this ruddy war is over
And we come back from Germany.
Roll on, when we go on furlough ;
Roll on, when we go on leave,
Then we'll catch the train for Blighty,
Though we'll leave the girls bereaved.

## GASSED LAST NIGHT

Later that night, very late it was, the nurses came in and several doctors, the beds were turned down and later the convoy arrived. I can see them now, about 30 of them all blindfolded with hands on each others shoulders filing down the marquee and the nurses and doctors breaking them up as they came to their respective beds, poor devils. I tried to see what was going on at the far end, then the sister said something to one of the nurses, both turned to look in my direction and within minutes I was given a drink from a feeding cup and two tablets. I couldn't see any more, I was off in a deep sleep, that was my lot.

It must have been early morning when I awoke and remembered the scene of the night before. Every bed was empty and at the foot of each bed was a urine bottle half full of pink urine, yes they had all been gassed, blind and died, but what of the horror never seen.

*from Tom Green's Journal*

## NOT SO LUCKY

I got a whiff of gas on the Somme, and had trouble with my throat and voice-box, but was told that the disability did not interfere with my work. True: I only had to stop work when feeling choked. Of course I have no work now; and no disability-pension.

*F. Gill*

## ENOUGH

All countries engaged in the war had periods of widespread mutiny, a fact which should be noticed and recorded, not hushed up. It took them all differently, according to their national characteristics. With Germany it was a continuous filtering-through of individuals or small parties who very logically concluded that they would be better off as prisoners in British hands than as combatants. In France, more spectacular defiance of orders paralysed initiative on two notable occasions. In Russia, the slow awakening of the peasant had the well-known results. In Italy it was a continuous corruption and lassitude that left the troops in the line provisioned with chestnut flour only. With the British, as might be expected, it occurred at the great base camp at Etaples, over some rumoured disagreement with the police. I never knew the truth, and perhaps no one does. For some days, a great docile mob walked about the streets completely out of hand, relatively harmless, and eventually returning to camp to be fed. Shortly after, the miserable failure of an offensive was brought to a close. But the effect was permanent. From this time there developed a new spirit of taking care of one's self among the men, which ended, in late 1918, in a few rifles being fired, and would, in a few more weeks, have meant the cessation of the War, by the front line not refusing but quietly omitting to do duty. The Armistice came just in time.

*R. H. Mottram*

# ROLLING HOME

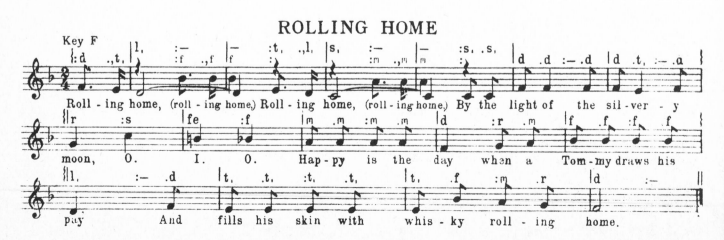

# KAISER ABDICATES

---

## IMPERIAL AND PRUSSIAN THRONES RENOUNCED

---

## CROWN PRINCE ALSO GOES.

### HAND HIM OVER!

The Kaiser is in Holland. More than a hundred years ago Napoleon was in Elba. From Elba Napoleon came forth, relighting the fires of destruction, troubling all Europe again, till he and all his mischief were extinguished at Waterloo. The moral is plain. It is our business to call upon the Dutch Government to surrender the troubler of the world into our keeping, and with him any other of the brood who are now or may be hereafter in their territories. We must run no risks. We cannot afford to have the earth-fire that we have extinguished with our agony kindled anew. A million British lives have been spilt in the terrible struggle. They did not grudge the sacrifice, those men who died for us. But the awful offering is finished; it must not begin again. The Kaiser and his tribe must be brought to judgment and at least held in safe keeping, lest the whole world perish.

## VICTORY PARADE

My mother made us little khaki uniforms. The buttons had naval anchors on them, which annoyed my brother and me; but there were no small military buttons available.

We put them on when the war ended and kicked the nursery wash-tub, which was known as Kaiser Bill.

'Kaiser Bill's dead,' we shouted.

There was to be a great parade through Rickmansworth to celebrate the victory.

We would wear our uniforms and wave small Union Jacks.

But what would our elder sister wear? Girls couldn't wear uniforms.

'I'll make her a dress out of Union Jacks,' my mother suggested.

We were disappointed when this turned out to be a joke and Betty appeared in an ordinary little girl's dress.

We sat on a garden wall near where the War Memorial now stands and waved our flags and cheered as the soldiers in khaki and hospital-blue marched past.

Britannia, in a flowing white robe and carrying what looked like a pitch-fork, rode on the local fire-engine pulled by two horses.

It was a splendid end to the war.

*Peter Tewson*

## THE ROAD BACK HOME

One platoon passed, the ranks close, a second, a third. Then a space. More space. Could this be a whole company? Three platoons? God! how terrible these men looked!—gaunt, immobile faces under shrapnel helmets, wasted limbs, ragged, dusty uniforms. . . . Did they still carry terrible visions of battle in their minds, as they carried the dust of the mangled earth on their garments? The strain was almost unbearable. They marched as though they were envoys of the deadliest loneliest, iciest cold. Yet they had come home; here was warmth and happiness; why were they so silent? Why did they not shout and cheer; why did they not laugh?

The next company advanced. The crowd thronged forward again. But the soldiers trudged on rapidly, doggedly, blindly, untouched by the thousand wishes, hopes, greetings which hovered round them. And the crowd was silent.

Very few of the soldiers were wearing flowers.

The little bunches which hung on their gun-barrels were faded. Most of the girls in the crowd were carrying flowers, but they stood trembling, uncertain, diffident, their faces pale and twitching, as they looked at the soldiers with anxious eyes. The march went on. An officer was carrying a laurel wreath negligently, dangling it in his hand, hunching his shoulders.

The crowd pulled itself together. A few hoarse shouts were heard, as though from rusty throats. Here and there a handkerchief was waved. One man murmured, convulsed: 'Our heroes, our heroes!' They passed on, unmoved, shoulders thrust forward, their steel helmets almost hidden by bulky packs, dragging their feet, company after company, little knots of men with wide spaces between. Sweat ran from their helmets down their worn grey cheeks, their noses stood out sharply from their faces.

Not a flag, not a sign of victory. The baggage wagons were already coming in sight. So this was a whole regiment!

*Ernst von Salomon*

172

# TIRED

This then, was the end. Visions of the early days,
their hopes and ambitions, swam before his eyes.
He saw again his pre-historic howitzer in the orchard
at Festubert, and Alington's long legs moved
towards him through the trees. He was back with
the Australians in their dug-out below Pozieres. He
saw the long slope of the hill at Heninel, covered
with guns, ammunition dumps, tents and dug-outs.
Ypres, the Salient, Trois Tours, St. Julien—the
names made unforgettable pictures in his mind.
Happy days at Beugny and Beaussart, they were
gone and the bad ones with them. Hugh was gone,
and Tyler and little Rawson; Sergeant Powell, that
brave old man; Elliot and James and Johnson – the
names of his dead gunners strung themselves
before him. This was the very end. What good
had it all been? To serve what purpose had they all
died? For the moment he could find no answer.
His brain was too numb with memories.

'Mr. Straker.'

'Sir.'

'You can fall the men out for breakfast. The war
is over.'

'Very good, sir.'

Overhead the pigeons circled and wheeled.

*F. Lushington*


# THE FORGOTTEN

Was anything happening now because our own men
had anguished through four months of incompetent
leading a year ago, or were going on endlessly, from
one battle to another? The agony represented by
the aggregate of Shaiba and Ctesiphon and the
coutnless combats in the twenty miles before
Kut, was immense. But it was a drop in the agony
of Europe, no one heeded it, it was right that no one
should heed it, for it was of no importance. It did
not matter how many thousand men died there, what
battles were fought and won.

*Edward Thompson*


## High Wood

Ladies and gentlemen, this is High Wood,
Called by the French, Bois des Fourneaux,
The famous spot which in Nineteen-Sixteen,
July, August and September was the scene
Of long and bitterly contested strife,
By reason of its High commanding site.
Observe the effect of shell-fire in the trees
Standing and fallen; here is wire; this trench
For months inhabited, twelve times changed hands;
(They soon fall in), used later as a grave.
It has been said on good authority
That in the fighting for this patch of wood
Were killed somewhere above eight thousand men,
Of whom the greater part were buried here,
This mound on which you stand being . . .
                              Madame, please,
You are requested kindly not to touch
Or take away the Company's property
As souvenirs; you'll find we have on sale
A large variety, all guaranteed.
As I was saying, all is as it was,
This is an unknown British officer,
The tunic having lately rotted off.
Please follow me – this way . . .
                    the *path*, sir, *please*,
The ground which was secured at great expense
The Company keeps absolutely untouched,
And in that dug-out (genuine) we provide
Refreshments at a reasonable rate.
You are requested not to leave about
Paper, or ginger-beer bottles, or orange-peel,
There are waste-paper baskets at the gate.

PHILIP JOHNSTONE
*1918*


# THE ROAD BACK HOME

On 11th November we marched back fifteen miles
to Bethencourt. A blanket of fog covered the
countryside. At eleven o'clock we slung on our
packs and tramped on along the muddy *pave*. The
band played, but there was very little singing.
'Before a man comes to be wise, he is half dead
with catarrhes and aches, with sore eyes, and a
worn-out body.' We were very old, very tired, and
now very wise. We took over our billets and
listlessly devoured a meal. In an effort to cure our
apathy, the little American doctor from Vermont
who had joined us a fortnight earlier broke his
invincible teetotalism, drank half a bottle of
whisky, and danced a cachucha. We looked at his
antics with dull eyes and at last put him to bed.

*Guy Chapman*

173

## HOMES FIT FOR HEROES

I don't know which was the worst, the war or the events which followed, with unemployment and even ex-Officers selling matches in Oxford Street. I hope that bloke in Salonika and the other bloke with his 'orse were amongst them. Yes, it was all over at last and when in 1919 I looked at my father and brother and our two rooms which measured 14 feet by 14 feet each and housed a family of eight, I said 'Tom your king and country need you'.

*from Tom Green's Journal*

## A BIT COMPLICATED

I have been granted the War Widow's pension; I am sure chiefly due to you. It was back-dated, but they kept £100 of the back money because I cannot have a retired pension as well. It is now straightened out, and they have sent me £3.15s balance from the £100, and I have to pay income-tax out of this; but I am very pleased. What is left is more than ever my husband got.

*F. W.*

### Estimated number of limbless war pensioners on 31st December, 1973

| Nature of Limb Amputation | Former and 1914 Wars |
|---|---|
| One Arm .. .. .. .. .. | 1,542 |
| Two Arms.. .. .. .. .. | 3 |
| One Leg .. .. .. .. .. | 3,409 |
| Two Legs .. .. .. .. | 105 |
| One Arm and One Leg .. .. .. | 14 |
| Multiple .. .. .. .. | 1 |
| Totals .. .. .. | 5,074 |

APRES LA GUERRE. — M⁰ HERPICT. "ALL READY FOR INSPECTION, MY DEAR!"
WINNING THE WAR (SECOND) SERIES. — N° 1 — 8ᵗ HQ. 1ˢᵗ CO.
GUARD ROOM.

### "REVENGE FOR 1919."

COPENHAGEN, Sunday.

The signature of peace caused little stir among the excitable Berliners.

The *Deutsche Zeitung* publishes an excited article under the heading, "The German People's Revenge," saying: "Now the honour of Germany is buried, and only through incessant toil will the German people be able to attain again their place among the nations. Then will come the revenge for the disgrace of 1919."

As a result of this article the paper has been suppressed by the Government.—Exchange.

Herr Hermann Mueller and Herr Bell, the Hun signatories to the Treaty, in a joint statement said:—

"We are signing without mental reservation, and what we are signing we will carry out. The German people will use every means in their attempt to meet the terms of the Treaty.

"Germany will make every effort to prove herself worthy of entry into the League of Nations."—Exchange.

### THE LIGHTS OF LONDON.

#### STRANGE EXPERIENCES OF LAST NIGHT.

Never has an illumination been more striking in its effects than was London' last night. Many have been more brilliant in the old days before the war, when coal, gas, and electricity had not become precious possessions carefully to be hoarded. Last night, however, it was possible for the first time for many a dark night to pass along the main streets of the capital in the full glare of arc lights and street standards. The sensation on stepping out of a side street still obscured in the dim glimmer of the war epoch now past and gone was almost uncanny.

It had been known that the signing of the armistice would be the signal for lights up, and within a quarter of an hour of the firing of the maroons men were at work, even in the distant suburbs, scraping the blacking off the lamp glasses. Had the public not become so hardened to war restrictions that they found it difficult to believe their severity could be so quickly relaxed every window blind would have been up in the London area last night. Many were.

Some of the great hotels had flaring braziers lighted outside their premises, and Piccadilly once again was the great White Way. It was possible to walk up the street—but for the crowds—and read a newspaper comfortably. It was natural that the crowds should frequent these brilliant avenues and shun the ill-lighted streets as relics of the past.

The official permission was announced in instructions telegraphed by the Home Office to the police authorities.

#### STREET LAMPS.

Every one watched for the searchlights, but only one or two were visible, and they soon ceased their efforts.

Masking of street lamps may be removed, but in view of the coal shortage the total number of lamps in use must not exceed one half the normal.

Shading of lights in houses and shops may be withdrawn, but the prohibition of lights in shop windows and of advertisement lights must be maintained on account of the coal shortage.

Fireworks displays and bonfires will be permitted by the military authorities for one week, subject to approval of the arrangements by the police.

Sale of fireworks for authorised displays permitted, but not the general use of fireworks by the public at present.

Restrictions on the ringing of bells and the striking of public clocks at night are withdrawn.

The President of the Board of Trade also announces that the operation of Part III. of the Lighting, Heating, and Power Order, 1918, relating to hotels, restaurants, clubs, and places of entertainment will be suspended during the present week. The effect of this will be that the prohibition on the serving of meals at hotels and restaurants after 9.30 p.m. and the closing of places of entertainment at 10.30 p.m. are temporarily suspended.

DR. LLOYD GEORGE TO GERMANIA

"The stains are ineffaceable, but you may save your actual life by eliminating from your blood the virus of Hohenzollernism, and by submitting to an inoculation of the Allies' prescribing."

| WAR BILL, £30 700,000,000. | |
| --- | --- |
| **ALLIES.** | |
| Great Britain | £8,700,000,000 |
| France | 4,000,000,000 |
| America | 3,000,000,000 |
| Italy | 2,000,000,000 |
| Japan, Belgium, Serbia, etc. | 750,000,000 |
| Russia | 2,000,000,000 |
| Total Allied cost | £20,450,000,000 |
| **FOES** | |
| Germany | £7,500,000,000 |
| Austria | 2,250,000,000 |
| Bulgaria and Turkey | 500,000,000 |
| Total enemy cost | £10,250,000,000 |
| Grand total | £30,700,000,000 |

## This Generation

Their youth was fevered – passionate, quick to drain
    The last few pleasures from the cup of life
Before they turned to suck the dregs of pain
    And end their young-old lives in mortal strife.
They paid the debts of many a hundred year
    Of foolishness and riches in alloy.
They went to death; nor did they shed a tear
    For all they sacrificed of love and joy.
Their tears ran dry when they were in the womb,
For, entering life – they found it was their tomb.

OSBERT SITWELL

## HERE'S TO THE NEXT TIME

A League of Nations can be no success—it cannot even be begun, it can hardly be thought of—unless you are going to have all the nations of Europe parties to it. If Germany were excluded, or if Germany were not welcomed into it with open arms—(Hon. Members:"Oh oh!" and "Never!") Yes, I say, with open arms—(An Hon. Member: "Remember the *Lusitania*!")—if you are going to have a League of Nations you must make up your minds that Germany as well as ourselves—(Hon. Members: "Never!")—must be welcomed.

Mr. G. Faber: Would you shake her bloody hand?

Mr. Lambert: Because, unless you do, you are merely perpetuating the old trouble of two great armed camps in Europe. You will have that trouble all over again. The whole basis of the League of Nations, the absolute foundation of it, must be that all nations are party to it. I do most earnestly ask the House not to be carried away by the raw passions, which I know are natural. Do not let us be carried away by our passions at the present time and take a view which I think is more likely to militate against the future peace of the world, and which most certainly cannot possibly assist towards ending this terrible War.

*Mr. Richard Lambert, Parliamentary Debates*

## Aftermath

*Have you forgotten yet? . . .*
For the world's events have rumbled on since those gagged days,
Like traffic checked while at the crossing of city-ways:
And the haunted gap in your mind has filled with thoughts that flow
Like clouds in the lit heaven of life; and you're a man reprieved
　　to go,
Taking your peaceful share of Time, with joy to spare.
*But the past is just the same – and War's a bloody game . . .*
*Have you forgotten yet? . . .*
*Look down, and swear by the slain of the War that you'll never forget.*

Do you remember the dark months you held the sector at Mametz –
The nights you watched and wired and dug and piled sandbags on
　　parapets?

## LAST WORD

I must tell you this, over that Court Martial in
the 1914 war, I lost 6d. a day throughout the
second war. You wouldn't believe it, would you,
but it's true.

*from Tom Green's Journal*

### *from* STRANGE MEETING

I am the enemy you killed, my friend.

I knew you in this dark; for so you frowned

Yesterday through me as you jabbed and killed.

I parried; but my hands were loath and cold.

Let us sleep now . . .

*Wilfred Owen*

Do you remember the rats; and the stench
Of corpses rotting in front of the front-line trench –
And dawn coming, dirty-white, and chill with a hopeless rain?
Do you ever stop and ask, 'Is it all going to happen again?'

Do you remember that hour of din before the attack –
And the anger, the blind compassion that seized and shook you then
As you peered at the doomed and haggard faces of your men?
Do you remember the stretcher-cases lurching back
With dying eyes and lolling heads – those ashen-grey
Masks of the lads who once were keen and kind and gay?

*Have you forgotten yet? . . .*
*Look up, and swear by the green of the spring that you'll never forget.*

SIEGFRIED SASSOON
*March 1919*